SKELETON

CHURCH

A BARE-BONES DEFINITION OF CHURCH

JEREMY MYERS

SKELETON CHURCH:
A Bare-Bones Definition of Church
(Close Your Church for Good: Preface)
© 2012, 2016 by Jeremy Myers

Published by Redeeming Press
Dallas, OR 97338
RedeemingPress.com

ISBN: 978-1-939992-45-1 (Paperback)
ISBN: 978-1-939992-14-7 (Mobi)
ISBN: 978-1-939992-15-4 (ePub)

Learn more about Jeremy Myers by visiting RedeemingGod.com

All Scripture quotations are taken from the New King James Version*. Copyright © 1982 by Thomas Nelson, Inc. Used by permission. All rights reserved.

TAKE THE FREE
SKELETON CHURCH
ONLINE COURSE

Join thousands of others at
RedeemingGod.com/register/
to get the *Skeleton Church* online course for free

Thanks for reading!

Books in the *Close Your Church for Good* Series
Preface: Skeleton Church
Vol. 1: The Death and Resurrection of the Church
Vol. 2: Put Service Back into the Church Service
Vol. 3: Church is More than Bodies, Bucks, & Bricks
Vol. 4: Dying to Religion and Empire
Vol. 5: Cruciform Pastoral Leadership

Other Books by Jeremy Myers

The Atonement of God
The Re-Justification of God: A Study of Rom 9:10-24
Adventures in Fishing (for Men)
Christmas Redemption: Why Christians Should Celebrate a Pagan Holiday
Why You Have Not Committed the Unforgivable Sin
The Gospel According to Scripture
The Gospel Dictionary

All books are available at Amazon.com
Learn about each title at the end of this book

For all who follow Jesus into the world

TABLE OF CONTENTS

Gnostics of all periods take one look at the Church and say to themselves, "You mean this is it? You mean this is all there is? Only what a simple-minded woman or that acned kid can understand; only what that half-educated preacher is saying?" The ancient Gnostics concluded that either Christianity must be disconnected from this embarrassing base or else abandoned altogether.

—Philip J. Lee, *Against the Protestant Gnostics*

FOREWORD

The three basic questions about life which all humans ask (whether they realize it or not) are: Who am I? Why am I here? Where am I going?

In seeking to define the church, this book answers all three questions. More than that, we will see that the church is God's answer to all three questions. The church is not just some loose-knit group of people who occasionally sit in a building on Sunday morning to sing songs and listen to a sermon. No, the church is God's plan for the world, and until each church member recognizes this, they will forever be wondering "Who am I? Why am I here? Where am I going?"

But once you understand who you are as a member of the church, you will discover that you are part of a story which spans from eternity past to eternity future. You are part of special people, with a special purpose, and called to a special task.

So are you ready to find out who you are, why you are here, and where you are going? If so, you must begin with gaining the barebones definition of church.

CHAPTER 1

SKELETON CHURCH

*In many areas, the Church today is encased in rigid insti-
tutional structures which impede growth. Perhaps 80 per
cent of such structures are not formal and official, but are
simply traditional and cultural. In the United States, for
example, few if any denominations have adopted an article
of faith stating that worship services must be held between
ten and twelve o'clock on Sunday morning—and yet this is
one of the most rigid institutional patterns of American
Christianity. In many areas, the same thing applies to lit-
urgy, the decision-making process, ideas about the "clergy,"
and even methods of evangelism. Much of this is simply
tradition; only a small percentage is a part of official
church polity. And yet it is precisely this traditional, only
half-perceived part of the church structure which is most
rigid, most resistant to change, and often most deadening
to the Church's life.*
—Howard A. Snyder

In Sedlac, Czech Republic, there is a Skeleton Church. It is made
from the bones of about 50,000 skeletons. Upon entering the
church, you are confronted with tens of thousands of skulls, skeletons, and bones. The walls and ceiling are covered with them. A gi-

ant bone chandelier hangs from the ceiling. The pulpit and baptistery are decked out with skulls. For the average person, entering such a building is a frightening experience.

When I first saw pictures of this building, I immediately thought, "Imagine the board meeting where this decoration plan was discussed!" I can hear it now: *Next on the agenda ... church decorations. We have two proposals before us. We can go with stained glass, marble tile, and flowers, or the second option, skulls and skeletons from ten thousand dead people.*

What were they thinking?

Well, the truth is that, as with most things in church, it just kind of "happened" over time. The church was originally a monastery with a cemetery nearby. In 1278, the abbot of the monastery travelled to Palestine and returned with some dirt from the hill of Golgotha. He sprinkled this dirt in the cemetery, and when word of his actions spread, the cemetery became a popular place for people to bury their loved ones.

Around the year 1400 a Gothic church was erected within the cemetery and something had to be done with all the bones that were unearthed during construction. The bones could not be discarded or burned, for this would show dishonor for the dead. So the bones were stacked in a lower chamber of the chapel. Over the years, the cemetery had to be expanded several times, and frequently, in times of war and during the bubonic plague, mass graves were dug and thousands of people were buried at one time. Frequently, old graves were dug up to make room for new burials, and again, all the old bones were stacked in the chapel.

Eventually, in 1870, a woodcarver was hired to put some order to the mass of bones, and from them he created massive bone archways, garlands of skulls, and a chandelier which contains at least one of every bone in the human body. In recent years, the church has become more of a tourist attraction than anything else, and has been featured in various movies and documentaries.

THE CHURCH OF BONES

This is somewhat like a lot of our churches today. Even if we don't decorate with bones, we are still surrounded by the memory and tradition of people long dead who have bound us into a frequently frightening tradition. And sometimes, it does get downright scary.

Try to get the pews out of your church when they've been there for 80 years and were donated by the saintly grandmother of Elder John and you will see how quickly the fangs and claws come out. Or, to see blood really begin to pour, suggest to the board that the church sell the building once and for all.

I once suggested this when I was interviewing for a pastoral position in a church. The elders told me they wanted their church to start reaching the lost, and were looking for a pastor who could lead them in that direction. "It's possible some drastic changes will be necessary," I told them. "Are you ready and willing to do whatever it takes to reach others with the Gospel?" They assured me that they were.

So I continued. "Let's say that after much prayer and careful discussion, the elders decided that to reach the community with the Gospel, God wanted us to sell the church building."

Silence. Crickets chirped in the background.

Finally, one elder spoke up. "Well, that would never happen. The building is an essential part of our ministry."

So I tried again. "But you said you were willing to do *anything* to reach your community with the Gospel. So what if the elders unanimously agreed, after much prayer and discussion, that one of the things God wanted you to do was sell your building? Is that something you'd be willing to do?"

The same elder spoke up again. "We would never come to that agreement. We need our building to reach our community with the Gospel. How could we reach the community if we didn't have a building? We're willing to do anything to reach the community, but the things we want to do in the community require a building."[1]

The interview moved on and it was no surprise when they didn't call me back for a second interview. I share this event here as one example of how churches are constructed out of dead bones. We are so often tied to the traditions of the past that these traditions become dead bodies around our necks, dragging us down into inertia. We cannot see past the bones.

It is not just with the traditional ways we do things, but also with the traditional things we believe. Challenge a Southern Baptist church on the ordination of women, a Reformed Church on Calvinism, or a non-denominational church on their independence, and see how fast the fangs are bared. In the early years, Christians used to kill each other over similar matters. We don't physically kill each other today, but sometimes the words we use can actually cause a more painful death than a sword.

All these fights and quarrels among Christians, however, are mostly about dead men's bones. They are arguments about the traditions of people who have gone before us which—although they remind us of who we are and where we have come from—make the church little more than a sideshow for bored tourists or a graveyard

[1] I write more about church buildings and their role in the church in my book, *Church is More than Bodies, Bucks, & Bricks* (Dallas, OR: Redeeming Press, 2014).

through which people aimlessly wander. The church has taken a valley of dry bones and raised it up into a building, but it is still only a building of dry bones. Even though the bones now have structure, they are still dead.

GIVING LIFE BACK TO BONES

It's not that bones are bad. Bones are good when used properly. Without bones, life would be impossible. But problems arise in life and in church when bones and traditions lose their purpose, and start to pile up and gather dust. Piles of dead bones and old traditions are not life-giving; they are life-threatening.

The solution, however, is not to throw out the bones. Instead, they need to be resurrected.

Thankfully, we serve a God who specializes in resurrection. He loves to bring the dead and buried back to life. He loves to bring order from chaos, light to darkness, and breath to dirt.

But even God, before resurrection can happen, must first reconstruct the old jumbled piles of bones into skeletons. Remember Ezekiel's vision of the Valley of Dry Bones? In Ezekiel 37, God shows the prophet a large valley filled with old bones. Ezekiel sees the random mass of bones come together in thousands of skeletons, and once constructed, they are covered with sinew and flesh, and only then does the Spirit of God bring new life to the skeletons, and they rise up into a great multitude of living people. In the passage, the bones represent the nation of Israel and how they have lost their hope and have been cut off from their land and the promises of God.

The point of the vision is that death is not the end, but is the place from which God can begin to restore life and resurrect old bones.[2]

I believe the same thing can happen to the church.

DRY BONES CHURCHES

Before God can bring new life to the church, we need to see it for what it often is: a valley of dry bones, a skeleton church, filled with piles of dusty old bones. And though there is much activity in the church today, most of it seems to be driven by media, money, and marketing. Are such things the signs of new life being breathed into the church by the Spirit of God, or are they just the creations of an old woodcarver rearranging the bones into chandeliers, garlands, and archways?

I believe much of the activity in the church today is not the Spirit of God moving among the church, but is little more than a woodcarver rearranging stacks of bones. However, taking the image of Ezekiel 37 as a guide, seeing a church of dry bones does not mean the church is dead, but is rather on the verge of being resurrected to new life. But before that can happen, the dry bones must come together. The bones of the church must be constructed into a skeleton.

This book is about constructing a skeleton for the church. The ideas presented in this book are the bare bones basics for the church. This book is not about the flesh, sinews, and muscle, for I believe that such things will vary widely from place to place and from time to time. Just as in life, one body varies greatly from the next, so also

---

[2] I write more about this idea in my book, *The Death and Resurrection of the Church* (Dallas, OR: Redeeming Press, 2013).

in the church. One local body will differ vastly from any other body. But in life, as in churches, the skeleton remains the same. This book does not tell you how to do church, or what your church should look like. It simply constructs a skeleton. It lays a framework. It does not attempt to address issues of leadership and government, or the proper order of services and programs. This book neither defends nor attacks the house church or the mega church, the organic church or the corporate church.

This book simply attempts to define and defend an internal structure for churches of all shapes and sizes, of all models, of all forms and denominations, and of all theological persuasions. It attempts to provide a skeleton, and nothing more.

My goal is the development of unity within the church. Most church arguments of the past 1700 years have focused on externals such as buildings, music preference, leadership styles, and a whole host of other church trappings. These are like arguing about which skin color, body type, hair styles, and clothing designs are best. While humankind has argued about such things in the past, we are hopefully coming to finally see past all the externals, and view each other as human beings. And that is how it should be for the church as well. We must learn to look past all the external trappings which make one group of believers different from another, and see that underneath it all, there is a similar structure, and a similar foundation for us all: the skeleton of the church.

Essentially then, this book is an attempt to provide a definition of the church that fits every church, from every age, in every culture, of every size, shape, and denomination. Whether you participate in a home church of 10 people, or gather in a mega-church of 10,000, there is an underlying structure that binds us all together. It is this underlying structure this book seeks to uncover and explain.

And though it takes some explaining, we will see that the church skeleton is quite simple. God intended church to be simple so that it could adapt and flex to fit any culture in any location at any time. We begin to see this when we understand the bare-bones definition of the church.

DISCUSSION GUIDE FOR
CHAPTER 1: "SKELETON CHURCH"

See pictures of the "Skeleton Church" in the Czech Republic and interact with others who have read this book by accessing the following online lesson:

https://redeeminggod.com/lessons/skeleton-church/

Study Questions

1. Are you willing and ready to do whatever it takes to reach others with the Gospel? Even if it meant selling your church building or selling your home? *That would be tough — Ordelheide's made that sacrifice,*

2. In this chapter, Jeremy proposed that much of the activity in *I would find it diff in giving up church as it* the church today is little more than a woodcarver rearrang- *is part of family &* ing stacks of bones. What do you think of this statement? *community of fellow believers of jesus to me.*

3. This chapter proposed that every church has a skeleton, and the things that create disunity in the church are like the outer appearances of our bodies ... skin color, hair styles, and clothing type. Do you think this truth can help bring about unity in the church? Why or why not?

Application: Before moving on to the next chapter, imagine what you would include in the bare bones basics of every church in every culture throughout all time.

CHAPTER 2

DEFINING CHURCH

Although ekklēsia is from the very first a secular and
worldly expression, it expresses the supreme claim of the
Christian community in the face of the world.
—*K. L. Schmidt*

Have you ever wondered why your church does certain things a certain way, while the church across town does everything so different? Churches have wide diversity, from music and preaching styles, to building construction and leadership approaches. Why is this? Some of it has to do with traditions and customs, but even these are often guided by something much more basic: the definition of the church.

What the church is supposed to be and do depends on how you define "church."

But getting a definition for church is not as simple as finding a verse in the Bible, asking your pastor, or looking one up in a theological dictionary. Though pastors and theologians often have definitions of church, these definitions tend to be full of complex ideas and theological jargon which require further explanation. For example, a typical definition of "church" reads something like this:

Church (Gk. *ekklēsia*) is the universal body of believers that functions under the headship of Jesus Christ and meets regularly in local assemblies to carry out the Great Commission through observing the ordinances of Baptism and the Lord's Supper and listening to the preaching of the Word of God, all for the edification of the believer and the evangelism of the world.

It is difficult to disagree with such a definition, but maybe this is because the definition is hard to understand. A few simple questions about this definition reveal how little it says:

- How can the church be both universal and local?
- Who is a believer?
- What do they have to believe and who gets to decide?
- What does it mean for Jesus Christ to be the head?
- Should we have pastors and priests or not?
- Why are baptism and the Lord's Supper called ordinances?
- What kind of baptism is required?
- How and when should people be baptized?
- What exactly constitutes "the Lord's Supper"?
- How often should it be observed?
- Who gets to do the preaching?
- How long should the preaching be?
- What does it mean to preach "the Word of God"?
- What about church leadership, organization, church government, denominations, our role in politics, and many other issues that are important to the average church?

Theology books generally attempt to answer these sorts of questions, and before you know it, an attempt to understand what the church is and what the church does requires detailed knowledge of dozens of books and an advanced educational degree or two. The "basics" of church seem to require a lot of advanced study and research. Apparently, the basics are not so basic after all.

CYCLES OF RENEWAL

Understanding "church" wasn't always so complex. Christianity began quite simply. It had simple ideas, simple structure, and simple beliefs. This simplicity allowed Christianity to spread rapidly, and gave early Christians the freedom and flexibility to adapt Christianity to any people and culture they encountered. Yet over time, as the Gospel spread and adaptations were made, questions were asked about which changes went too far. As these questions were asked and answered, traditions were formed and creeds were created. Simplicity, creativity, and flexibility were abandoned for philosophical complexity, centralized control, and standardized form. Everybody had to live the same way, believe the same thing, and follow the same leaders.

After a while, Christianity became so complex that it opened the door for a renewal movement—a return to simplicity. The renewal movement focused on simple beliefs and simple practices which can be quickly taught and learned. This allowed the new movement to spread rapidly, as Christianity did at first. But over time, this renewal movement gained its own complexities, traditions, and accepted leaders, until it became so complex that a new renewal and return to simplicity was required.

When and where did this renewal cycle take place? It has actually happened numerous times over the past 2000 years. The cycle from simplicity to complexity and back to simplicity happens sometimes in individual churches, and other times in international movements which span a century or two. Most decent books on church history recount several such cycles of renewal.

When these cycles are studied, it becomes clear that one of the things all renewal movements have in common is an emphasis on freedom. The more complex a religious system becomes, the more it enslaves the people who are part of it. What begins as an innovative idea or celebration becomes a mandatory belief or tradition that must be practiced if one wants to be accepted.

A renewal movement tries to slough off all these manmade requirements, and return to the freedom and simplicity at the center. Those who are involved in the movement believe that the Scriptures contain few specifics about how the church functions. In other words, the Scriptures provide very little instruction about when and where the church should meet, what it should do when it meets, how it is governed, and a variety of other questions that consume the thinking of the average Christian.

The Scriptures do explain, however, what the church is. As long as we understand this, we can be as free, flexible, and creative as we desire when it comes to what, when, where, and how the church functions. This simple definition of church will be introduced below, and then defended and clarified in the next three chapters.

EKKLESIA

Defining "church" begins with defining *ekklēsia*, the Greek word for "church." The word literally means "gathering" or "assembly." By itself, the word has no spiritual connotation. In Greek usage, it was frequently used for any type of gathering, whether social, political, or religious, and even for groups of people that never actually "gather."[1] Since *ekklēsia* has such diverse meanings, how is it that the early church came to adopt it as the word to describe the followers of Jesus as a group?

Some say that Jesus used the word Himself in Matthew 16:18, and so He is the one who chose this word. This is possible, but it is also likely that Jesus spoke in Hebrew or Aramaic, in which case, *ekklēsia* is still a translation of what Jesus actually said. But even if Jesus Himself used the word *ekklēsia*, we still have to ask why He chose this word, and not some other word which could have been used to identify the followers of Jesus.

Robert Farrar Capon believes that the early believers and New Testament authors adopted *ekklēsia* as the preferred term in four steps:[2]

1. In the Hebrew Scriptures, two major words are used to refer to the *congregation* of Israel, or the *assembly* of Israel—that is, to Israel itself as a *community*. They are *qāhal* and *ēdah*.

2. During the postexilic period, the Hebrew Scriptures are translated into Greek. This Greek translation of the Hebrew Scriptures are known as the Septuagint, or LXX (Roman numerals for seventy). Though Hebrew was still used, many of the Greek-speaking Jews and most of the Gentile converts to Judaism (and later, Christianity) used the LXX as the preferred way of reading the Hebrew bible.

---

[1] This, and much of the following information on *ekklēsia* is from K. L. Schmidt, *"kaleō"* in *Theological Dictionary of the New Testament*, Vol. 3 (Grand Rapids: Eerdmans), 501-536. See also P. T. O'Brien, "church" in *Dictionary of Paul and His Letters*. Gerald F. Hawthorne, Ralph P. Martin, Daniel G. Reid, eds. (Downers Grove, IL: InterVarsity), 123-131.

[2] Robert Farrar Capon, *The Astonished Heart* (Grand Rapids: Eerdmans, 1996), 36-37.

3. In the LXX, two Greek words are generally used to translate *édah* and *qáhal*: *édah* is generally rendered *synagōgē*, and *qáhal* as *ekklēsia*.

4. When the early New Testament church cast about for a word to describe itself as the fulfillment of the *community*, the *congregation*, the *assembly* of Israel as the people of God, it had to make a choice between *synagōgē* and *ekklēsia*. Since the word *synagōgē* had been preempted by becoming the name of a particular institution within Judaism (the *synagogue*), that left them with only *ekklēsia* as the term to designate themselves as the fulfillment of the destiny of God's people.

Capon is certainly right about how *ekklēsia* came to be the preferred term, but why was it ever translated as "church" rather than as "gathering" or "assembly"?

In the early history of the church, when the New Testament was being translated from Greek into Latin, there was no clear equivalent in Latin for *ekklēsia,* and so various terms were proposed. Tertullian used *curia* ("court") while Augustine famously wrote of the *Civitas Dei* ("City of God").

One surprisingly common term used by various Greek writers was *thiasos* ("party"), which generally referred to a group of revelers marching through the city streets with dance and song, often in honor of Bacchus, the god of drunkenness. Another Latin term used from time to time was *circus,* which means "circle" or "ring" and was also used of the bloody and brutal gladiatorial games of ancient Rome. Why this term was used is hard to discern. Is it because Christians were often the fodder for lions and swords in such games? Or is it because "church gatherings" seemed raucous and disorganized to outside observers, sometimes bordering on frenzy like the crowd at gladiatorial games? Maybe it was the emphasis in "church" on the blood of Jesus which reminded some of the cry in the coliseum for the blood of the victims.

The point is that many early Latin writers did not know how to translate or describe the Greek term *ekklēsia*, and they used a wide variety of words. The terms they proposed offer tantalizing clues as to how the church functioned and was viewed during its early years, but there is little consistency among the various writers.

So let us move on to the English word "church." Where did this word come from? The most likely source seems to be that it is derived from the German *kirche*, which in turn comes from the Greek adjective *kuriakos*, "belonging to the Lord" (cf. 1 Cor 11:20). This Greek adjective is a derivative of *kurios* ("Lord") and since Christians generally met on "the Lord's Day," the first day of the week, it made sense to call them *kuriakos*, the Lord's people. So "church" probably came from the German *kirche* and the Greek *kuriakos*, but is not an actual translation of *ekklēsia*.

So in the end, it seems best to side with what Robert Farrar Capon argued above. The New Testament writers borrowed *ekklēsia* from the Septuagint, where the people of Israel are often referred to as the *ekklēsia* of God. The Israelites were called and gathered by God from the world to accomplish a specific purpose and task. So also, the writers of the New Testament believed that the *ekklēsia*, the people whom God has gathered in their day, were also put together for a specific task and purpose.

What was this task and purpose? It was the purpose God had given Israel, and the purpose for which Jesus lived and died: to be a blessing to the world, bringing a message from God about hope, love, forgiveness, and grace.

DEFINING CHURCH

This is a long way to travel to find a definition of church. But we have seen that "church" itself is not the best translation of *ekklēsia*, and *ekklēsia* itself is a borrowed word from Hebrew which described Israel as the people of God on earth whom He chose to accomplish His mission.

So maybe that is how best to approach the definition of "church." Not by defining the words themselves, but by looking at the entire flow and structure of the grand story in Scripture. As we do this, we can work toward a biblical definition of "church."

It becomes immediately clear that the church is not a building, a place, a function, or an event. It is instead, a gathering of people by God. They are not necessarily gathered in a physical location, but are gathered spiritually into Jesus Christ. Since they have been gathered into Jesus, they are to follow Him by doing what He did and continues to do in the world. This is why God chose Israel to be the people of God, and why God has chosen Jesus to be both the climax and the new beginning for God's next stage in accomplishing His mission on earth.

So then, perhaps a concise working definition of church is as follows:

> **The church is the people of God**
> **who follow Jesus into the world.**

This definition fits with the definition of *ekklēsia* and what seems to be God's plan in Scripture and throughout history. This is what Jesus taught His disciples about why He came and what He wanted them to do once He left. This is what Paul and Peter continued to teach and write as they went into the world to carry on the mission of Jesus. It is what nearly every spiritual renewal movement in history has emphasized and tried to recover. It is simple, easy to remember, and avoids some of the technical jargon and theological baggage inherent in many other definitions.

This definition can fit with nearly every form and style of church, whether it is liturgical or contemporary, mega-church or home-church, denominational or independent. This definition can be applied to all types of churches in all cultures throughout time. This definition can apply to your church, as will be explained in the next three chapters.

DISCUSSION GUIDE FOR
CHAPTER 2: "DEFINING CHURCH"

Interact with others who have read this book by accessing the following online lesson:

https://redeeminggod.com/lessons/defining-church/

Study Questions

1. Give your definition of church.

2. Describe how most of our church practices and church theology came about. What do you think of this?

3. Where does the word "church" come from?

4. What do you like or not like about the author's definition of church?

Application: Take some time this week to really think and dream about what you would like to be doing for Jesus. If there were no limits, no time constraints, and money were no object, what would you most like to be doing for Jesus?

PEOPLE OF GOD

To say "the people of God" is to think primarily in terms
of salvation history.
—*Eduard Schweizer*

There are numerous terms that could have been used in reference to
the church, such as Temple of God, Holy Nation, Royal Priesthood,
Citizens of Heaven, God's Building, and others.

In *The Astonished Heart,* which is an excellent book about the
church, Robert Farrar Capon discusses some of the terms that have
been used throughout history: the Brethren, the Disciples, the Way,
the Believers, and the Fellowship.[1] However, the three that will be
discussed below are the most common in the minds of people and in
Scripture. These three are: the Body of Christ, the Family of God,
and the People of God. In this chapter, we will look at how each of
these terms are used in Scripture, and why "People of God" seems to
be the best way to describe and identify the church. Though the other images for the church have benefits, the "People of God" is the
best image for the church.

---

[1] Robert Farrar Capon, *The Astonished Heart* (Grand Rapids: Eerdmans, 1996),
34-37.

THE BODY OF CHRIST

When people think of biblical imagery for the church, the most common picture that comes to mind is the Body of Christ. Yet while this phrase is found a few times in Scripture (e.g., Rom 7:4; 1 Cor 10:16; 12:27; Eph 4:12), all except one refers to the actual body of Jesus, rather than to the church. And although body imagery is found somewhat frequently in Paul's letters (cf. Rom 12:5; Eph 1:22-23; 5:23; Col 1:24; 2:17), only one text, 1 Corinthians 12:27, refers to the church specifically as the Body of Christ.

Paul may have selected body imagery for the church due to the similarities between the Greek concepts of body (Gk. *sōma*) and the church (Gk. *ekklēsia*). For example, *sōma* is a word which represents a person in their totality. It is understood that the *sōma* has parts, some physical (bones, flesh, blood), some spiritual (soul, spirit), and some psychological (emotions, intellect, will, personality), but the word does not refer to just one of these parts, such as the physical, but to the entire person. This is like the church, the *ekklēsia*. The church is a unified whole, and while it is made of numerous members, does not refer to one member only.

Nevertheless, although the image is a good one, it is used only by Paul, and even then, less frequently than other imagery. Since this is so, how is it that the idea of the church being a Body became so prominent if it is not found throughout the New Testament, but only rarely in Paul's letters? How did it become the most popular and widely known image for the church? It is probably a result of the dual emphasis in many churches on the teachings of Paul and the gifts of the Holy Spirit. These twin factors converge in passages that picture the church as a Body, and so in the minds of many, the Body is the main image for the church. One of the most common passages which supports this image is 1 Corinthians 12.

1 CORINTHIANS AND THE BODY

The primary passage from Paul that talks about the gifts of the Holy Spirit is 1 Corinthians 12. In this chapter Paul compares the church to a body, and just as each part of a body has its own unique function, so also our gifting by the Holy Spirit provides each person a unique purpose within the church, which is the Body of Christ (12:27). To understand Paul's idea in 1 Corinthians 12, some background is necessary. As noted above, the vast majority of the uses of the word "body" (Gk. *sōma*) in the New Testament are by Paul. Of these, he uses it most frequently in the letter of 1 Corinthians. Why?

The Corinthian Christians saw themselves as spiritually elite. They were super spiritual. For them, everything was about the Holy Spirit and their own spiritual life. Many of them were beginning to neglect the physical reality around them, and even deny that what was done in the flesh had any serious ramifications upon their spirit. In their minds, the flesh and the spirit were separate. This error of dualism has its origins in the philosophical ideas of Plato. Much of Paul's letter to the Corinthians is focused on correcting this hyper-spiritual outlook on life. He attempts to show that what is done in the flesh has serious ramifications for life in the Spirit.[2]

This is part of the reason Paul emphasizes the image of "body" so much in his letter to the Corinthians. He wants to show that what is done in the body affects not only the spirit, but also the body. And

---

[2] I will eventually post my commentary on 1 Corinthians at www.gracecommentary.com.

not just the physical body, but also the entire Body of Christ, the church. In other words, the earth-shattering concept that Paul emphasizes to the Corinthians is not only that the physical and spiritual side of a person are connected in one unified body, but also that each and every person within the Body of Christ is connected to each other. Therefore, when one person sins in the flesh, the entire Body of Christ is dragged along as well.

One example is sufficient to show Paul's thought. After an extended discussion of why the Corinthians should glorify God with both body and spirit, Paul tells the Corinthians in 1 Corinthians 6:15-20 that having sex with a prostitute is not simply a sin of the flesh, but also engages the spirit. And since the church, the Body of Christ, is spiritually connected, when a man unites with a prostitute, it is not just with his own body and spirit that unite with the prostitute, but the Body of Christ and the Holy Spirit as well! Paul argues that such an idea should be enough to keep us from this sort of sin, and indeed, all sin.

So when Paul begins to emphasize in chapter 12 the image of the church as the Body of Christ, his readers will have understood that they are all in this together. What one person does spiritually or physically, is done to all. If an action spiritually or physically harms one, it harms all. If it benefits one, it benefits all. Paul's emphasis in 1 Corinthians 12 is that as members of the Body, we are connected to each other. Each person has a unique purpose and function within the Body to fulfill, which, if carried out, benefits the individual and the rest of the Body.

This idea continues on through chapters 13 and 14, and is climaxed in chapter 15 with Paul's discussion of the resurrection. Paul's point in this entire section is that the church is a unified whole, which he calls the Body of Christ. The Body is a community of people in Jesus Christ. "The Body of Christ is precisely the Church in which Christ moves out into the world."[3] In the words of K. L. Schmidt, "Christ is the church itself, for this is the Body of Christ."[4] Such an understanding is surprisingly similar to what was seen in the discussion of *ekklēsia* above. The church consists of those who have been gathered by God into Jesus Christ. Therefore, the church—Body of Christ—is Jesus Christ to the world. All who are gathered into Jesus are part of Jesus, and participate with Jesus in what He does in the world.

So the church as a Body is not a tradition to be followed or an office to be filled, but is rather the total, unified whole of all who are in Christ. Everyone is equal within the Body, and everyone has a part to play. At the same time, all actions, behaviors, and beliefs of one part affect every other part. Though the Body is not an individual person, each individual within the Body must understand that their actions have consequences, not just for themselves, but for the entire church. This is the point Paul seeks to drive home here in 1 Corinthians, and in other letters as well (cf. Rom 12:4-8; Eph 4:12-16).

So the picture of the church as the Body of Christ is an excellent image, and is probably the most common image in the mind of most Christians today. However, although it is a good image, it is not the only image for the church, nor is it the most common. The concept of the church as the Body of Christ is found in only a few places within the writings of Paul. Therefore, another image should be used which more widely represents the entire Bible.

[3] Eduard Schweizer, "*sōma*" in *Theological Dictionary of the New Testament*, Vol 7 (Grand Rapids: Eerdmans), 1080.

[4] K. L. Schmidt, "*kaleō*" in *Theological Dictionary of the New Testament*, Vol. 3 (Grand Rapids: Eerdmans), 509.

FAMILY OF GOD

The most common image for the church in the New Testament is that of the church being a family. As a result, many think of the church as the "Family of God." Yet while family imagery is everywhere, the exact term "Family of God" is never used. First Peter 4:17 comes close in speaking of the "household of God" and Ephesians 3:15 speaks of the church as being the whole family in heaven and on earth, but the church is nowhere specifically referred to as the "Family of God."

Nevertheless, the church as a family is a common image and illustration for the church. The authors of Scripture frequently use imagery about believers being related to one another as brothers and sisters, fathers and mothers, and all of us together being children of God. Husband and wife imagery is also common, with the husband, or groom, representing Jesus Christ, and the bride, or wife, representing the church (e.g., Matt 25:1-13; Eph 5:22-33). Many passages describe God as our Father, and Jesus as our Brother (cf. Mark 3:31-35). So since the concept is so widely used, it is quite valid to think of the church as the Family of God.

Aside from its frequency, the image of church as the Family of God is quite useful as well. First, as with the image of the Body, the image of Family has a lot of similarities with the definition of *ekklēsia.* Just as the church, the *ekklēsia,* is ultimately a spiritual gathering, whether or not it ever gathers physically, so also, a person is part of a family even if they rarely, if ever, have a family reunion. A person is part of the family simply by being born into it. Even if a member is physically absent from the rest of the family for months or years, they remain part of the family. Thinking of the church in this way is very helpful in understanding how the church can exist as a spiritual unity without ever completely coming together in a physical location.[5]

Thinking of the church as a family is also extremely helpful when it comes to church governance, organization, leadership, decision-making, titles, discipline, use of money, and basically every other matter related to how a church functions. Many today have questions about how a church should operate. Thinking of the church as a family helps clarify most of these issues.

- *Who should lead in a church?* Who leads in your family? How did they get this position? Do they have a title that you must call them?
- *When you get together as a church, what do you do?* What do you do in your family?
- *How should a church spend money?* How does your family spend money? Do you ever give money to other families? If so, who, and why do you give money to them?
- *How does church discipline function?* How does discipline work in a family?

Answers to these sorts of questions vary from family to family, but that is okay, since variety is also in the nature of families. So also, answers to these questions will vary from church to church, but that is also okay, since variety and diversity is within the nature of the church.

So the image of church as the Family of God is everywhere in Scripture, and is extremely helpful in understanding the nature of the

[5] For a detailed description of the family as a framework for church government and roles, see R. Banks, "Church Order and Government" in *Dictionary of Paul and His Letters.* Gerald F. Hawthorne, Ralph P. Martin, Daniel G. Reid, eds. (Downers Grove, IL: InterVarsity), 131-137.

church and how it should function. Nevertheless, it is not the term used in our proposed definition for the church because the concept of family does not usually include the vital function of mission that should be inherent within the church. The idea of family, while ideal for describing relationships and fellowship, lacks the element of mission to the world. And mission is why the church exists. So a term that includes the concept of mission without neglecting the idea of relationships is necessary.

PEOPLE OF GOD

The term "People of God" seems to be the best way of identifying the church. It includes the elements of connectivity and relationship that are inherent within the terms "Body of Christ" and "Family of God," but also contains an element of mission and purpose within God's plan for the world. Also, the term and its related concepts are found throughout Scripture; not just in the New Testament for the church, but also in the Old Testament for Israel.

In the Old Testament, "the people of God" is one of the primary ways of referring to Israel. It emphasizes the familial relationship of the Israelites as God's children, as well as the governmental connection of God as the King and Ruler of Israel. They belong to Him both as His family and as His subjects. The idea of Israel as the people of God is also present in the New Testament, but it is expanded to include the church. Or rather, maybe it would be clearer to say that the idea of "church" includes all the people of God, both Jew and Gentile. In writing to the church, Peter says that once we were not a people, but now we are the people of God (1 Pet 2:10). In context, Peter's point is that everything that God accomplished in the world through Israel is now going to be accomplished in the world through the church. We are, Peter says, the new priesthood, a holy nation, a chosen generation, a new people of God.

This does not mean that God has replaced or rejected Israel. It simply means, as Paul points out in Romans 11, that Gentiles have been grafted in to the people of God, so that God's church, God's chosen people, now includes both Jews and Gentiles.

The grand narrative of Scripture is that God, since the beginning of time, has drawn out of the world a people for Himself who will carry out His mission by being a blessing to the world. In times past, He used an ethnic nation of people. Today, He uses people from all nations and countries who are gathered together into Jesus Christ as the church, the People of God.

Seeing this theme within Scripture helps explain why God chose Abram out of all the people of the world, why He blessed Isaac over Ishmael, and Jacob over Esau. They were not chosen because they were better or because they were His "favorites." No, God chose so that they would bless others. This is the mission of God. It is why He raised up and rescued Israel from Egypt. It is why God sent judges, kings, and prophets. It is why Jesus Christ came, lived, served, died, and rose again. It is why the church was formed. The People of God throughout Scripture have been a chosen vessel to accomplish God's will in the world.[6] We will return to this theme frequently in the rest of this book since, if we are not being a blessing to the world, then we are not living as the People of God.

The term "People of God" includes not just the church, but also the nation of Israel in the Old Testament as the people of God. And inherent within the term is God's plan in human history to restore

---

[6] See Christopher J. H. Wright, *The Mission of God* (Downers Grove: InterVarsity) for a detailed explanation of this Scriptural theme.

and redeem mankind. Thus, "People of God" is a missional term. It is a term which reminds us that God is on a mission in the world and He is using a particular people to carry out this mission. The other terms for "church" do not carry this connotation, and so "People of God" seems to be the best image for thinking about church. It is used everywhere in Scripture, carries the helpful image of connectedness and relationships, and is filled with the concept of God's mission in the world.

PEOPLE OF GOD'S KINGDOM

Before we close out this chapter, it is helpful to note that the term "People of God" is closely related in Scripture to teachings on the "Kingdom of God." The two ideas almost coexist. For example, without people to inhabit it, there would be no kingdom. And the kingdom advances only through its people. To put it another way, the People of God are the People of God's Kingdom. The People of God are citizens of the Kingdom of God.

But what is the Kingdom of God? The Kingdom is what Jesus inaugurated. He did not inaugurate a religious movement or community. He inaugurated the Kingdom of God. He teaches over and over in the Gospels that with Him, the Kingdom has begun. Yes, a day will come when Jesus Christ will physically return to reign over the entire earth for 1000 years, but this does not mean that the Kingdom has not yet been inaugurated. This idea is confusing to some, who think that if the Kingdom is a time when Jesus rules over all, then the world should be a place of peace, kindness, generosity, and love.

The confusion begins to fade when we think of the Kingdom of God as the Reign of God. The Kingdom of God is present anywhere that the Reign of God is present. The Hebrew parallelism of the

Lord's Prayer reveals that the kingdom comes wherever the will of God is done (Matt 6:10). Based on this truth, we must pray for the will of God to be done on earth just as it is done in heaven. And so logically, if the Kingdom is present wherever God rules, and He rules in heaven, then the Kingdom is active in heaven. Furthermore, if we are to pray for the reign of God on earth (and by inference, actively work for this prayer to be answered, cf. Matt 6:33), then whenever and wherever God reigns, the Kingdom is there also.

So the Kingdom of God is only present with the People of God. The two are intricately connected. Each depends upon and requires the other.

Again, the Kingdom is quite similar to the church. Just as the church goes where its people go, so also, the Kingdom of God goes wherever the People of God introduce the reign of God. It is not a future hope which awaits our death and resurrection. The Kingdom of God is partially a present reality which can be experienced and shared right now, as we live with each other according to Kingdom ethics and principles.

> A truly biblical ecclesiology should focus not so much on the fact that the church is the community of the saved but that the church is the community of those who, being redeemed through the cross, are now to be a kingdom and priests to serve God and to reign on the earth.[7]

This brings us back again to the missional idea that is inherent within the term "People of God." The term does not just identify a people; it also identifies their task. The people of God are to live out

---

[7] N. T. Wright, *Evil and the Justice of God* (Downers Grove: InterVarsity, 2006), 139.

the reign of God in their lives and among the other people of this world. This is the subject of the next chapter.

DISCUSSION GUIDE FOR
CHAPTER 3: "PEOPLE OF GOD"

Learn more and interact with others who have read this book by accessing the following online lesson:

https://redeeminggod.com/lessons/people-of-god/

Study Questions

1. Why did Paul use "the Body of Christ" as an image of the church?

2. What are the benefits of thinking about the church as "the family of God"? What are the drawbacks to this image?

3. Why is the term "People of God" the best descriptor for the church?

Application: As you go about your life this week, try to think of yourself in relation to your identity as a member of the "People of God." Don't identify yourself as a citizen of the United States (or whatever country you reside in), or as a person of a particular class, race, demographic, or political party. Instead, just think of yourself as a member of the "People of God." Then watch what this does to your outlook on current events.

CHAPTER 4

FOLLOW JESUS

The church can't rise because it refuses to drop dead.
—*Robert Farrar Capon*

Why does God gather a people for Himself? Is it simply because He can? No. The People of God are gathered for a reason. They are gathered for a purpose. The beginning of that purpose is found in the ministry of Jesus Christ. The People of God are gathered to learn from Jesus, to follow Him, and to be like Him. The bones of the skeleton church are not gathered together by some random woodcarver, configured in ghastly nightmare of skulls and bones. No, the People of God are formed by a carpenter, Jesus Christ, to be His glorious image in the world. Jesus is the one shaping the church, and He forms it in His own image. To see what the church must be, we need only to look at Jesus. When we look at Jesus, we see a vision for the church.

LIVING THE GOSPELS

This vision for the church in Jesus Christ begins with reading the Gospels properly. Many people read about Jesus in the Gospels through a faulty paradigm. They read the Gospels to find out what

Jesus did and said, and then, based on what they discover, try to do and say similar things as Jesus. While this is close to how we should read Scripture, it is off in one major point.

We are not to read Scripture to see what Jesus said and did so that we can say and do it too. Instead, we are simply to read Scripture so that we can see what Jesus said and did. That's it. Don't take it further. The Gospels are a beautiful, transforming story all by themselves. They are inspiring. But if we are tempted to take the next step of trying to copy and emulate what we read within the pages of the Gospels, we end up killing the message and the inspiration of Scripture. When we try to take the stories of the Gospels and find their moral message to apply it to our lives so that we can be like Jesus, we lose the force, the impact, and the importance of the story. We moralize the life out of it.

We also moralize Jesus to death by trying to "apply" what we read in the Gospels to our own lives. But Jesus did not come to be the moral to a story. He came to be the Way, the Truth, and the Life of this world. If we think He is just good for some sermon application and trite examples on how to live life, then we will never experience Him as He intends.

Which is why the majority of the church is little more than a stack of dry bones. We are looking to the Bible for life, but life is not found in the Bible. Life is in Jesus Christ Himself (John 5:39). If we look to the Bible for life, we will find only more dry bones. But if we let the stories within Scripture become our lifeblood, and our soul, they transform us into Who God wants us to be. And God does not want us to be Abraham, Moses, David, the prophets, the apostles, or Paul. We are not these men, and God does not want us to become those men. The same is true of Jesus. We are not Jesus, and God does not want us to try to become Jesus. By this, I mean that we are not supposed to be Jesus of the first century AD, a Jewish Rabbi who walked around the Judean wilderness healing others and teaching people about the Kingdom of God. We don't need that kind of Jesus today, and God does not want that kind of Jesus today, and we should not try to be that kind of Jesus. Do not misunderstand! We desperately needed Jesus as He was and as He came! I would not want it any other way. But it is a mistake to think that every person, every age, every generation, every location must try to replicate the ministry of Jesus in our day and location. Jesus did what He did and where He did it because that was what He wanted to do in that time and in that place.

But He does not want to do the exact same things in our time and in our places! He wants to do different things. Better things. Wonderful things. He may even want to do some similar things. But He will not do identical things.

The stories of Jesus in the Gospels are the stories of Jesus in Israel during the first century AD. But in twenty-first century New York, or twenty-first century London, or twenty-first century Hong Kong, Jesus wants to do new things and different things. Some of the things He did in Israel 2000 years ago may look similar to what He wants to do today, but they will not be identical. He still wants to teach, and heal, and feed, and love, but in ways that fit our times and cultures. And what He wants to do in Hong Kong will look different than what He wants to do in London just as both will look different than what He already did in Jerusalem. The stories of the Gospel provide inspiration, guidance, and a push in the right direction, but they do not provide explicit instructions which must be replicated in every time and culture.

And how is Jesus going teach, and heal, and feed, and love others today? How is He going to do this in New York, and London, and

Hong Kong? Through the church. Though His people. Through the People of God.

This is why we do not read the Gospels to find out what Jesus did so we can reproduce it. No, we read the Gospels to find out what Jesus did. Then we read our own lives, and our own times, and our own culture, and we listen to the prompting of Christ within us, and try to understand what Jesus wants to do in the world today. In this way, the Scriptures inspire us to attempt new things and serve in new ways that maybe the Scriptures themselves never talk about.

The Scriptures are filled with numerous attempts at describing how this works and what it looks like. One popular idea in Paul is that of being "in Christ" or Christ being "in you" (e.g., Rom 12:5; 2 Cor 2:14; 5:17; Gal 3:28; Col 1:27). We also read about being the servant of Christ (1 Cor 4:1), the workmanship of Christ (Eph 2:10), and numerous other ideas and titles. The point of all these myriad of ideas is that Jesus is still at work in the world through us. He is returning in and through us. The bones of the church have been gathered to be Jesus in the world.

The early church tried to live out this vision, and the book of Acts shows many of the new directions which the apostles took as they tried to follow Jesus. They were not trying to replicate the ministry of Jesus again, but were trying to do similar-but-different things in their towns and cities. They read the Scriptures for inspiration, prayed for guidance, sought wisdom from one another, and then stepped out in faith to see where Jesus would lead.

This is what it means to follow Jesus. We are not retracing His steps from 2000 years ago. We are following where He leads *today* (cf. John 10:27). What does this look like? Let us begin with a term that most people are familiar with: discipleship.

DISCIPLESHIP TODAY

Generally, when someone describes the action or process of following Jesus, they use the term "discipleship." This is a good term, and is one of the words used in Scripture to describe our relationship to Jesus in this world. However, the term has lost most of its meaning and significance over the years, and usually means something today that it did not mean during the lifetime of Jesus.

Today, when people hear the word "disciple" they think of a "student" or "pupil." These actually are synonyms for the word, but being a student or pupil today looks very different than it did in the days of Jesus. Today, we think of a classroom setting, where one person stands up front and lectures, and everybody else sits dutifully in chairs or at desks and soaks in the knowledge from the teacher, usually taking notes and writing down what is said.

This is the primary way students learn today, and so we get the idea that if being a disciple of Jesus means being a student of Jesus, then being His disciple means studying Him. We think that good disciples are good students. They read the Bible, attend Bible study, memorize Bible verses, listen to Bible sermons, and read books about the Bible. They take notes, and underline verses in the Bible, writing important insights into the margins. The really advanced students learn Hebrew and Greek so they can study the Bible in the original languages.

But this is not what it meant in the days of Jesus to be a disciple, or student.

Two words in the New Testament are translated as "disciple." The first is *mathētēs*. The word does mean "learner, student, or pupil" but this looked very different in the first century than it does today. While there was "classroom time" it was always punctuated and followed by time out in the streets and marketplaces of the community, putting into practice what had been learned in the "classroom."[1] It was often thought that the primary teaching actually took place, not through the lecture, but out with the people, as the students followed their master's example in loving and serving the people of the town. It would be very close to what we would think of as "apprenticeship." The student learns a skill from the master in four stages: First, he listens to the master's instructions. Second, he watches the master perform the action. Third, he performs the action with the master's help. Fourth, he is able to perform the action on his own, and starts teaching it to others. A *mathētēs* who only listened to the master teach, and never progressed out of the classroom, would never be able to adequately function in society.

The second word which is often translated as "disciple" is *akoloutheō*. Only the verb form is found in the New Testament, which expresses an action. The root meaning is "path" and implies following behind or accompanying somebody. Once again, there is no idea in this word of a passive pupil sitting in a chair soaking up the words of a teacher week after week after week. Teaching is involved, but practice is the main pursuit.

So discipleship in the New Testament era is not equivalent to how it is often portrayed today. Today, someone is considered to be a good disciple if they attend all the church services, take notes on all the sermons, read all the best Christian books, listen to sermons on the radio, memorize Scripture, have daily devotions, and go to a

---

[1] I write about this more in my book, *Cruciform Pastoral Leadership* (Dallas, OR: Redeeming Press, 2017).

weekly Bible study. Someone who did this in the New Testament era would be commended for their dedication to Scripture study, but they would not be called a disciple. A disciple was someone who actually did something with what they learned, and did it in a way that resembled their master (cf. Luke 6:40). So being a disciple of Jesus implies more than just learning about Him, but trying to actually be like Him in our own time and culture. Since the word "disciple" has lost most of this meaning, I prefer to use the term "following Jesus" as it tends to include this quality of movement.

THE ESSENCE OF FOLLOWING JESUS

As I have indicated above, following Jesus is not just about doing the same things He did in His life and during His ministry. While following Jesus does imply the action of being like Jesus, it does not mean we are to be exactly like Him. Some speak and write about "being Jesus" in the world, and while I agree with the idea, we must be careful about what we mean. We do not mean that we are to look and act exactly like Jesus. No, someone who tries to do that is not properly following Jesus, or even "being Jesus."

Some have pointed out that the word "Christian" means "little Christ" and while that is true, I do not think that God wants a bunch of little Christ's running around trying to do the ministry of God on earth. God does not want cookie-cutter Christ's all trying to look, talk, and act exactly like Jesus. God has brought together a diverse group of people into the People of God because God wants the church as the People of God to consist of a diverse group of people. But when we try to make everybody fit into a particular mold and shape because we think a particular way looks most like Jesus, we are not allowing the life of Jesus to fill the dry bones that God has gathered together, and are only trying to reshape and reform the pile of dry bones into something a little more organized. But it only ends up looking like death.

God has brought together a pile of dry bones so that it can be put together and assembled by Jesus and filled with the life-giving power of the Holy Spirit, not so that we can look and act exactly like the Jesus we read about in Scripture, but so that we can look and act like the Jesus that God wants to see in our world today.

Rather than asking ourselves, "What would Jesus do?" it is closer to the truth to ask, "What would Jesus do today? What would Jesus look like today? How would Jesus speak and act today?" We must not answer this question too hastily, for far too often we think that a Jesus of today would look and act and talk exactly like the Jewish Jesus of first-century Israel. But the Jesus of 2000 years ago looked and acted a lot like the average person of His day. Sure, He said and did some things differently, but for the most part, you probably would not have been able to pick Jesus out of a crowd. The same would be true today.

So when we follow Jesus today, we should not try to live and act and talk in a way that enables people to "pick us out of a crowd." Sure, we will do and say some things differently than the people of the world, but for the most part, we will look and act just like everybody else. When we follow Jesus, we are not trying to be the Jesus of 2000 years ago. That is not what Jesus wants. He wants us to be the Jesus of today, the Jesus of here and now, the Jesus of blue jeans and cellphones, that doesn't use religious jargon or hang out with only religious people.

When we follow Jesus, we will live in a way that does not destroy or hide our humanity, but amplifies and magnifies its. We will live in a way that fulfills the dreams and longings of all mankind, which bring into reality God's values and vision for this world. When we follow Jesus, we will be more human; not less. In this way, we will glorify God with our humanity because we are living as humans the way God intended humans to live.

The church is not an enclave of refugees *from the world;* it is the sacrament of God's presence *in the world* by the Mystery of the incarnation. It is not supposed to look as little like the world as possible but as much like the world as it can manage.[2]

This was the way of the early church. They blended in to the surrounding culture so perfectly, that simply by looking at them, you could not tell by dress or by speech who was a Christian and who was not. In the late second century AD, a Roman scholar and historian named Diognetus wrote about Christians in his day. Look at what he says set them apart:

The Christian cannot be distinguished from the rest of the human race by country or language or custom. They do not live in cities of their own; they do not use a peculiar form of speech; they do not follow an eccentric manner of life. ... Yet, although they live in Greek and barbarian cities alike ... and follow the customs of the country in clothing and food and other manners of daily living, at the same time they give proof of the remarkable and admittedly extraordinary constitution of their own commonwealth.

They live in their own countries, but only as aliens. They have a share

---

[2] Robert Farrar Capon, *The Astonished Heart* (Grand Rapids: Eerdmans, 1996), 114.

in everything as citizens, and endure everything as foreigners. Every foreign land is their fatherland, and yet for them every fatherland is a foreign land. They marry, like everyone else, and they beget children, but they do not cast out their offspring. They share their board with each other, but not their marriage bed.

They busy themselves on earth, but their citizenship is in heaven. They obey the established laws, but in their own lives they go far beyond what the laws require. They love all men, and by all men are persecuted. ... They are poor, and yet they make many rich; they are completely destitute, and yet they enjoy complete abundance.[3]

The early Christians set themselves apart from the world around them, not by looking different, talking different, or behaving different in any way, except in the behaviors which contradicted the values and goals of Jesus Christ. Christians were so well-blended into culture and society you could not pick one out of a crowd. It should be similar today. We must be differentiated from our culture, not by our t-shirts, jewelry, bumper stickers, haircuts, or Sunday activities, but by our love, generosity, service, and kindness toward all.

The Jesus of today looks very different than the Jesus of 2000 years ago, and Jesus wants all of us, together, as the People of God, *to be* the Jesus of today in this world. We are not a bunch of little Christ's running around, trying to look and act and talk like a bearded white-robed Jewish Rabbi. Instead, we must show the world what the love, mercy, grace, and forgiveness of the Kingdom of God looks like in our own time and in our own culture. Jesus was the incarnation of God; the church is to be the incarnation of Jesus.

---

[3] Cyril Richardson, ed., *Early Christian Fathers* (New York: Simon & Schuster, 1996), 175

THE INCARNATION OF THE CHURCH

Philippians 2 may be the most famous passage in Scripture on the incarnation of Jesus. The central point of this passage is that Jesus completely humbled Himself in becoming human, even to the point of submitting to death on the cross. But, says Paul, it was because of the complete humility of Jesus Christ, that God raised Him up and glorified Him above every name, so that at the name of Jesus, every knee will bow and every tongue confess that Jesus Christ is Lord.

As we seek to follow Jesus, one of the primary directions Jesus will lead us is into humility and death. If a person, organization, or group claims to be following Jesus, but is maneuvering for power, strength, position, authority, prominence, fame, and glory, this person or group is probably not following Jesus at all. He does not lead into such areas. If the Gospels and Philippians 2 have anything to say to us at all, it is that the way of Jesus in this world for those who follow Him is toward humility and death.

Even the concept of "following Jesus" implies a death to the past or a break with who we used to be. It is a change in direction, a shift in course, a new target and goal. "Following Jesus means self-denial, humility, poverty, suffering ... The term 'follow' is used elsewhere as in the pregnant sense of participation in Jesus' vocation to suffering and death."[4] This is not a popular message, but true discipleship of following Jesus into humility and death never is.

Our churches often try to sell discipleship as the cure-all pink and purple pill: "Take two of these, and everything that ails you will disappear! Jesus will fix your marriage, your job, your finances, and even

---

[4] Eduard Schweizer, *Lordship and Discipleship* (London: SCM, 1960), 15.

your car!" But this is exactly what discipleship is not. Real discipleship may lead to no money and no car at all. Setting out to follow Jesus is signing up for a suicide mission. If we follow Jesus to the end, we follow Him to death.

But this is not discouraging. Death is the only way forward. Jesus knew this, which is why He so resolutely faced the pain and suffering of crucifixion. He knew what so many of us today do not seem to recognize: death precedes resurrection.[5] We want the resurrection without the death. We pray for revivals and ask God to pour new life and new power into our churches and ministries, and God says, "I'm trying, but you refuse to die! I've tried to crucify your ministry so it can be raised in glory, but you put it on life support. Let it die! Kill it, if need be! Only then can you be raised to power and glory, so that through you and your ministry will every knee bow and every tongue confess that Jesus Christ is Lord." Only when we die and rise again in this way are we beginning to follow Jesus and be the incarnation of Jesus in this world.

As the incarnation of God, Jesus looked to the Father and only did what He saw the Father doing. As the incarnation of Jesus, we must look to Him to see what He is doing in our lives, our families, our neighborhoods, our communities, and our countries, and then only do what we see Him already doing. And when we do such things, it is actually Jesus who does these things in and through us.

We should not be surprised when He leads us in a direction that He did not go in the Gospels. We should not be shocked when wants to do things He did not do, and help people He did not help.

---

[5] I credit Robert Farrar Capon for this idea. See *The Astonished Heart* and pretty much every other book he has ever written.

The Gospels do not provide us with a cookie-cutter roadmap or a pattern to trace, but rather a trajectory to propel us forward in new directions and to new places. Some of it will be familiar to what we see Jesus doing in the Gospels, but it will never be identical. However, it will always be the same direction. Jesus is always moving further out and deeper in. When we follow Jesus, we follow Him, not away from the world, but more deeply into the world.

DISCUSSION GUIDE FOR
CHAPTER 4: "FOLLOW JESUS"

Learn more and interact with others who have read this book by accessing the following online lesson:

https://redeeminggod.com/lessons/follow-jesus/

Study Questions

1. What is the biggest mistake we make when reading the Gospels?

2. If Jesus is not asking us to duplicate His life, what is it we *are* supposed to be doing with our life?

3. What was the key element of discipleship in Jesus' day that is different from the way much of discipleship is practiced today?

4. What are the best ways to show Jesus to this world? What are the best ways to show others that we are followers of Jesus?

Application: Instead of spending time this week in Bible study, put that same amount of time into applying the Scriptural knowledge you already know. Specifically, go out and show love to someone, knowing that as you do, you are revealing Jesus to them.

CHAPTER 5

INTO THE WORLD

*When the church stops teaching and starts helping people,
listen and watch for the Rabbi. It changes our posture in
relation to the world.*

—Stephen Jones

So far we have seen that the church consists of the people of God who follow Jesus.

But where is Jesus leading? If we are following Jesus, He must be leading us somewhere.

Many say that we don't know where Jesus is leading, so we must blindly follow Him by faith. This is not true. Scripture is pretty clear about where Jesus is leading us. Yet most of us don't like the direction He's headed, so we claim ignorance. We feel that as long as we plug our ears and shout "LA-LA-LA-LA! I CAN'T HEAR YOU!" that Jesus will just leave us alone and we can go on sitting in our comfortable pews, hearing heavenly music and insightful sermons, all the while ignoring the promptings of the Holy Spirit and the voice of Jesus in our lives which is telling us to get off our butts and get out there into the mess and filth of life.

But it is not all our fault. The church has lied to us. Most of us think we became Christians so we can get our lives cleaned up. Then when Jesus tells us to go get dirty again, we think we must have heard Him wrong, and if only we read our Bibles and pray a little bit more, we will hear Him correctly. So we sit around, waiting to hear something that Jesus is never going to say.

And the longer we sit, the easier it gets to ignore the voice of Jesus. We begin to confuse the voice of Jesus with the voice of Satan. When on Sunday morning one voice says, "Go to church" and the other says, "Go hang out with your friend who got drunk at a party, slept with the wrong person, and now has AIDS," we think the first voice must be Jesus, because the second voice is not in alignment with what we've been told that good Christians do on Sunday.

Besides, we desperately want to listen to that first voice which tells us to attend more church services and Bible studies. That first voice is so much easier. Since the messiness of life is so difficult and tiring, the average church service offers a convenient way of escape. By immersing ourselves in Sunday services and weekly Bible studies, and telling ourselves that this is what it means to follow Jesus and be His disciple, we can sit around with our heads in the heavenly clouds, waiting for the rapture and entrance into heavenly bliss. Meanwhile, our friend with AIDS is contemplating suicide, but we will never know it because we were too busy learning the outline to Romans and how to practice contemplative prayer.

This is not what following Jesus is all about. It is not what He Himself did, nor what He taught His disciples. It also is not how He leads us today. No, when Jesus became human, He entered fully into the filth and stink of this world, not to bring judgment and condemnation, but to announce peace, forgiveness, justice, mercy, freedom, restoration, redemption, and joy! This is what He taught His disciples, and just as they had trouble with it, so do we. We are happy to follow Jesus into the world if we can condemn sinners, but when

Jesus sends us out to the ghetto with invitations to His party, we're not sure we want any part of that. So we go back to our padded pews, professional music, and preach-athon church conferences. These are so much safer and cleaner.

I sometimes picture Jesus charging out the doors of our churches, shouting "Follow Me!" Yet when He gets half-way down the block He looks back over His shoulder and says, "Where'd everybody go?"

Jesus wants to lead people into the world, and when the People of God follow Jesus, it is into the world that we must go.

INTO THE WORLD

When we follow Jesus, He leads us deeper into the world; not away from it. This initially confuses most of us, because we thought we were following Jesus to be freed from this world, and yet He wants to lead us right back into it! Isn't that where sin, the flesh, and the devil reign? Isn't the world under the control of the evil one? Isn't the world under the judgment and condemnation of God? Isn't Jesus just going to destroy it all anyway when He returns? Why would He lead us back there? We don't want to go back. We left it all behind so we could follow Jesus into peace and safety.

Nevertheless, it is into the world He leads us.

Why?

Why does Jesus lead His people back into the world?

It is because God has a plan for the church.

God did not form the church just because He could. He had a goal in mind, a purpose. God had a plan. This plan was revealed in Jesus, and was initiated by Jesus, but it was not finished or completed by Him. Yes, right before His death, Jesus declared "It is finished!"

but He was talking about His redemptive work on the cross, not the entire redemptive plan of God for the world. That task was only begun by Jesus and continues now in and through the church, the people of God. The work that Jesus began, we must continue. The plan of God, the direction of God, the goal of God for the church is that it continues to live and act like Jesus within the world. This is why God created and formed the church, so that we can continue to be Jesus in the world.

This is the central idea of John 17:14-16 when Jesus prayed that His followers would remain in the world, but not be of the world. Often, this gets interpreted in a way that calls us to abandon all connections to the world. People think it means that although we still live on earth, we really have nothing to do with what goes on here. Such an interpretation helps us grow in holiness and purity, but also causes us to lose all influence and effectiveness in bringing the rule and reign of God to earth.

Yet it seems that what Jesus is really praying in John 17:14-16 is that we be in the world, just as Jesus was, but not "from" it. That is, we are to be in the world as fully as possible, while not adopting the world's values and ways of doing things. We are to live and function in this world while not adopting the values of this world. We have a different value system, a different way of doing things, a way that follows the goals and values of heaven. And as we follow Jesus into this world, we live and emulate these Kingdom values, showing others that God's way of doing things is superior to the world's way. This is what it means to follow Jesus into the world by continuing His mission and spreading His values.

Note carefully that God's ways don't include speaking in Christian clichés, praying instead of helping, or sitting in padded pews instead of serving in the streets. These are not God's ways, but religious ways. God's ways are better, not because they insulate and protect the church from the world, but because they draw the church back into the world to be His representatives there. God's ways are better than the world's ways because His ways are more loving and forgiving. This is all seen as we look at the mission of Jesus.

THE MISSION OF JESUS

What was the mission of Jesus that He expects us to carry out in this world? What were His values that He wants us to emulate? When speaking of the mission of Jesus, most immediately think of the Great Commission in Matthew 28:19-20: "Go and make disciples of all nations ..." It is true that this is the mission which Jesus has given to His church, but as we saw earlier, few people today understand what it means to make disciples. Most of the time, we think it means gaining as much knowledge as possible about Jesus, God, and the Bible. While teaching is definitely *part* of the discipleship process, it is only a part. Jesus goes on to say that discipleship requires teaching others *to observe.* In other words, teaching them *to do* what Jesus said and did; not just teaching them to know about it.

Luke 4:18-19 is one of the places where we read about the mission of Jesus. In these verses, Jesus states that His goal and focus would be to bring the Year of Jubilee upon the earth, so that all debts are cancelled, all slaves are set free, and hope and healing is given to those who need it. Jesus sought to usher in an era of God's promised blessings being poured out upon the earth. In essence, Jesus declared that His work was to bring healing, liberty, freedom, restoration, and joy to this earth.

Since we are followers of Jesus, this too is our mission. Jesus began the mission, and then instructed us to carry it on. We are not here to become experts in the Bible or gain purity in our pews, but to follow Jesus in fulfilling His mission to the world. In his book, *Simply Christian,* N. T. Wright describes it this way:

> The church doesn't exist in order to provide a place where people can pursue their private spiritual agendas and develop their own spiritual potential. Nor does it exist in order to provide a safe haven in which people can hide from the wicked world and ensure that they themselves arrive safely at an otherworldly destination.
>
> The purpose [of the church] is clearly stated in various places in the New Testament: that through the church God will announce to the wider world that he is indeed its wise, loving, and just creator; that through Jesus he has defeated the powers that corrupt and enslave it; and that by his Spirit he is at work to heal and renew it.[1]

Jesus taught this message in nearly everything He said and did throughout His entire ministry. He came to this earth, not to provide a way for people to escape the planet and leave all the wickedness behind, but to provide a way for the redemption of the planet, and the transformation of all people upon it. Jesus does not invite us to follow Him so that we can sit around and wait until we die. No, Jesus invites us to follow Him so that we can actually live.

But how? What does this look like?

Well, the truth is that following Jesus into the world really doesn't look like much. To most people, it doesn't look like anything at all. And that is both the genius and the power of Jesus' way.

---

[1] N. T. Wright, *Simply Christian* (New York: HarperOne, 2006), 203.

SALT AND LIGHT

One of the metaphors Jesus used to describe how we work and function within the world is His picture of salt and light. Jesus said that His followers would be the salt of the earth and the light of the world (Matt 5:13-14).

In our churches, we accurately teach that in biblical times, salt was a preservative. And based on that fact, we think that Jesus is telling us we need to be the world's preservative. We need to defend and protect the culture and society against all decay and filth. We try to preserve what is good and upright in society and culture. We embark on political activism by endorsing pro-life, pro-family, and anti-homosexual political candidates. We picket the strip clubs and hold rallies to get prayer back in school. We write letters to the editor and rent billboard space on the interstate. We believe that it is the Christian duty to moralize the behavior of the world.

We do similar things with the image of light. We try to be as big and as bright as possible, thinking that this will draw people to Jesus and reveal the truth of God's Word. So we try to get noticed in the community. We "go big" and make a splash. We spend money on advertising, and do our best to match the glitz and glamour of Hollywood. We hope that if people notice us, and we can look popular and relevant, they will want to be part of us. But it rarely works. And so some churches go the opposite route, and simply try to burn the sin out of others. These churches seem to believe that if our holiness and righteousness can shine as bright and hot as the sun, then all evil within ten miles of the church will scurry back into the hole it came from. These churches think it is their job to point out every person's sin, shining the spotlight upon any who fall out of line, and in so doing, call people to repentance. But this rarely works either, and usually the only sin that gets revealed is the hypocrisy of the church. And really, the sin in society and culture just seems to grow. So churches redouble their efforts and either go bigger or shout louder. But nothing seems to slow this downward spiral into moral decay. Some critics of the church argue that the efforts of Christians have only exacerbated the decline.

It is probably time to recognize then, that the church has gone about being salt and light in the wrong way. We have tried to be noticed. We have tried to influence. We have tried to get into positions of leadership and power. We have tried to shout people into submission, and beat them into obedience. It doesn't work, and in fact, it turns out to be a complete misunderstanding of Jesus' metaphor about salt and light.

When Jesus teaches about salt, He says nothing about preservation. We are to be salt, but not to preserve. Though they did use salt to preserve food in the days of Jesus, there was another use for salt as well: Just like today, salt was used for flavor. It is the flavoring characteristics of salt that Jesus mentions in His metaphor.

And as a flavor, salt should not be noticed. It is there to enhance the flavor; not overwhelm it. Have you ever eaten a dish with too much salt? When I was younger, someone in the family made a batch of cookies and accidentally switched the sugar and the salt. Those cookies were not a family favorite. At the same time, when salt is called for in a favorite dish, but is left out, the dish tastes bland. Salt brings out the flavor in food, and shouldn't be noticed until it's gone.

The same is true of light. Light is helpful for life, but too much light is harmful. It should not be blinding, glaring, or harsh. But when the lighting is just right, you don't notice it until it is gone. In the teaching by Jesus, He talks about giving light to those in the house (Matt 5:15). Clearly, He is not talking about a light with the intensity of the sun. He is talking about a nice, warm fire in the hearth, or a few candles placed in strategic places around the room. They give off a nice glow and let people go about their work or leisure. The light goes unnoticed, without blinding or distracting those who are in its presence.

This is the way of the church when we follow Jesus into the world. We are present in all areas with others, working among them, eating where they eat, visiting the places they visit, enjoying the same activities. But we are a hidden influence. A small dash of salt, which goes unnoticed, but provides the spark of life and intensity of flavor which is missing when we are not around. We are a light, showing the way forward and guiding people onto the way of truth, whether they recognize it or not. When we are not around, things seem less clear. When we are salt and light, people cannot put a finger on why they want us around, but they know they do.

We must find the right balance between not enough and too much if we want to be salt and light. We need to exist in our communities in a way that helps them exist and function with all the flavor and color that God intended, but not in a way that we become distasteful or harsh. We need to exist in a way that is influential, but unnoticed. We need to exist in such a way that the only time we are really noticed is when we are gone.

So as we follow Jesus into the world, He pretty much leads us into the places where we are already living and working. He leads us over to the neighborhood diner, not to evangelize, but to eat and laugh with the regulars. He leads us down to the ball game, not to judge and gossip, but to cheer on the local team with our friends. We follow Him to our jobs, where we work as the most honest and diligent employees (or managers) the company has ever seen.

When we are ready, Jesus may lead us to other places as well. He might lead us over to our neighbor's house when his wife dies, not to evangelize or "share the gospel," but to sit and cry with him as he grieves. Maybe Jesus will lead us down under the bridge to bring tarps and potato chips to the homeless, or down to the street corner to hang out with the prostitutes while they wait for work. Again, none of this is to "fix" them, but to simply love them and show them that they have value.

In all of these situations, God is not calling us into these daily or dark places to correct behavior, or judge and condemn it. He isn't even calling us to go to these places to "evangelize," for that would do more damage than if we didn't go at all. Jesus is calling us to these places so that we might simply love and live with those who are there. We are to be a steady and pleasant flavor, a constant and hopeful light, and loving incarnation of our loving God.

FOR FREEDOM YOU HAVE BEEN FREED

Such an understanding brings great freedom and flexibility to our lives within the church. There are very few rules or requirements on how to be the church, or what to do as the church. During the ministry of Jesus, as He taught and modeled His principles of freedom, He had numerous encounters with the established Jewish religion of that day. Over the years they had developed over 6000 laws, rules, and regulations that governed nearly every aspect of life. And one of the things that Jesus taught was that He had come to bring freedom from such religious bondage. Jesus was not a fan of religion, and wanted to set people free from it (John 8:32-36).

Paul says much the same thing when he reminds his friends in

Galatia that they must not return to the religious chains that they had been freed from, but must remain free in the freedom they had in Jesus Christ (Gal 5:1).

People who seek to follow Jesus into the world must be allowed the freedom to investigate what this means on their own as they follow Jesus. Religious rules, regulations, and traditions should not restrict the person who follows Jesus in new directions to new places. And new places don't just mean unreached countries, but also people in our own neighborhoods and town who are overlooked and maybe even rejected by the other churches in town. Jesus is more likely to lead you across the street than across the ocean. In following Jesus, there is nothing necessarily sacred about salt water, and we may be surprised that when He leads, He does not take us very far.

And don't go looking for a roadmap before you agree to step out your door. The Bible does not provide one, and Jesus is not in the map-making business. Following Jesus into the world is not the type of adventure where all the questions can be answered up front. Questions like "Where will we go? What will we do? What will happen to us on the way?" are answered differently for each person, and often, only as they are following Jesus into the world.

DISCUSSION GUIDE FOR
CHAPTER 5: "INTO THE WORLD"

Learn more and interact with others who have read this book by accessing the following online lesson:

https://redeeminggod.com/lessons/into-the-world/

Study Questions

1. What places do you feel God leading you to go which you have disregarded thus far in life? Why have you not followed Jesus to these places?

2. What is the goal for God's church?

3. What does John 17:14-16 really mean for Christians?

4. What does it mean to be salt and light in this world?

5. From what did Jesus break our chains?

Application: When you hear that still, small voice urging you to do something else on Sunday or Wednesday instead of "going to church," don't ignore it. Instead, stop and consider if it Jesus inviting you to follow Him into the world. Maybe He wants to get you out of the pew and into life. If so, follow Him wherever He leads. Skip "attending church" for the reality of following Jesus.

CHAPTER 6

GET SOME FLESH
ON THOSE BONES

*The church should enable us to realize that we are at a
party of outrageous proportions; and it should make us
want nothing so much as to shout the invitation to that
party at the top of our voices.*
—*Robert Farrar Capon*

This book has attempted to show that the church consists of the
People of God who follow Jesus into the world. This is a simple,
memorable, and flexible definition of church which can be applied to
all churches, throughout time, in any culture and geographic region,
of every shape and size.

But a definition of church is not "church." It is just a definition.
It is a framework. A skeleton. And a skeleton, by itself, can do nothing. It just lies there. Worse yet, the definition proposed in this book
does not answer most of our questions about church. It does not explain the when, where, and how of church. The definition of church
proposed above does nothing to answer the questions we all have:

- When and where should the church meet?
- Who should be the pastor? Can the pastor be a "she"?

- What form of church government should we follow?
- Should we be independent or join a denomination?
- What should our service look like? How much music? What kind of music? How much preaching? What kind of preaching?
- What should our community involvement look like? Whom should we serve? When? How?
- Should we own a building? Should we rent?
- Should we start cell groups, Bible studies, and prayer meetings?

Many of these sorts of questions I seek to address in other volumes of the *Close Your Church for Good* series of books, but the basic definition of church provided by this book does not provide answers to these questions. It does, however, provide a framework upon which to build. The definition of the church is the skeleton of the church, and once the skeleton is in place, we can begin to add sinew, muscle, flesh, skin, hair, and finally, clothes. And once the skeleton is in place, and flesh has been added, God can breathe new life into that body, to live and function as the people of God who follow Jesus into the world.

THE BEAUTIFUL CHURCH

The beauty of this church God has created is that just as there are no two human beings on the face of the earth or throughout time who have been exactly identical, so also, there will never be two groups of believers which are exactly identical in all ways. Once we have the skeleton definition of church, we build on this skeleton by adding muscles, flesh, sinew, skin, hair, and clothes. How do we do this as the church? We add muscles by looking at the people in our local group and determining the strengths and abilities God has given to us. We add skin by looking at the culture which surrounds us and the personalities of the people who are part of our gathering. We get direction for our eyes, ears, hands, and feet by looking at the burdens and needs of our own people, and those in the surrounding community.

As we do this, the body which we form upon the skeleton church becomes beautiful, unique, and perfectly suited to be and do exactly what God desires in our community. And just as in life, our bodies change with time, so also, the group of believers we are part of will also change and develop with time. As new people come, and as other people go, new muscles will be added, others will be toned, and a few may cease to be used. The hair styles and clothing styles may change as people develop different tastes and habits. The things our eyes see and our ears hear may change as well, as new people lead our feet in new directions, and our hands to do new things.

But underneath all this change, and underneath all this diversity, the skeleton of the church stays the same. No matter how we look on the outside, no matter what we do, how we function, or where we go, underneath we are still the People of God who follow Jesus into the world.

So stop trying to resist change. Change is what happens as bodies grow. And stop trying to copy the church across town, or the famous church in another state. They have different flesh than you do, and their muscles, skin, eyes, hands, feet, and hair were given to them by God to accomplish what He wants in their town during this time. God has given your group different muscles, skin, eyes, hand, feet, and hair, which are perfectly suited to follow Jesus into the world in your neighborhood and community. If you try to copy the church across town, you will be like Michael Phelps trying to copy Nastia

Liukin. Michael was made for swimming, and Nastia for gymnastics, and both excel at doing what they are good at. But if Michael Phelps became jealous of Nastia, and tried to perform a layout backflip on a 4-inch balance beam, it would be painful to watch, and potentially life-threatening.

Yet both Michael and Nastia have roughly the same skeletal structure. Sure, there are some height differences and a few other things that set one skeleton apart from the other, but for the most part, their underlying structures are identical. But it would be a disaster for either one to try to live identically to the other. Instead, they have recognized the things that make them unique, and have focused on strengthening and honing those areas, and as a result, are able to accomplish what few others in the world can do. And both are breathtaking to behold.

So also with each local church fellowship. Each group of believers has an underlying skeletal structure which is identical to every other group of believers. We are all the people of God who follow Jesus into the world. But how this looks, acts, and functions in each particular setting will vary greatly. Some churches will be a Michael Phelps. Some will be a Nastia Liukin. Some might be an Albert Einstein, a Martin Luther King, Jr., or even a Chris Farley. But however God made us, He wants us to be "us." And when we do that as the church, we will be beautiful and successful in His eyes. We will be breathtaking to behold.

FREEDOM AND FLEXIBILITY

Once we understand that God is not as concerned with outward appearances and functions as He is with the interior form and structure, we are freed from numerous things that drag the church down. We no longer feel like we have to measure up to some other church. We no longer have to feel that there is one right way of doing things. We no longer feel the need to judge and condemn other churches for doing things differently.

When we view ourselves and all other groups of believers as one people of God who follow Jesus into the world, we can recognize that Jesus makes each group look different so that we can each follow Him in different ways, to do different things, in different places. Thinking this way about the church is liberating and freeing. We are free to be who we are. We are liberated to follow Jesus wherever and however He leads. If we see another church head off in a direction that causes us to raise our eyebrows, we can simply shrug our shoulders and say, "Well, Jesus has not led us in that direction" and leave it at that. We must answer to Jesus for how well we followed Him, for to our own Master we stand or fall (Rom 14:4).

As we begin to view the church this way, all the old questions, debates, and arguments fade away into insignificance. We stop focusing on what other churches are doing, and stop being so concerned about the "right way" of doing things, and focus instead on making sure our group is following Jesus into the world in the best way we know how. Once these arguments and debates fade away, the way is clear for the Spirit of God to fill our bodies with life, and to move us into the world with power, vitality, and joy.

Howard Snyder put it this way:

> Once these hindrances are removed—not only individual sin but also human traditions, worn-out structures, and fundamental misconcep-

tions about the nature of the Church—then the Church will grow through the power of God within it.[1]

How the church looks and how the church grows will be different in every generation, every culture, every age, and every country. It can even manifest wide diversity among different gatherings of believers within the same town. Not only is this diversity allowed within the People of God; it is expected.

IT'S ALIVE!

Do you want to be the church today? Stop focusing on what you think you are supposed to be doing. Stop looking at what other churches are doing. Instead, focus on your internal structure as the people of God who follow Jesus into the world, and then, based on the people within your fellowship, and their desires, talents, knowledge, gifts, and abilities, embark on an adventure that will transform you and your fellowship from a pile of dead and lifeless bones into a vibrant, creative, loving, and joyful church that draws people to Jesus simply by being fully alive. Do you want to be alive?

In the Foreword to this book, we learned that there are three basic questions every person is asking about themselves. These three questions are "Who am I? Why am I here? Where am I going?" Now that we have defined the church and seen how you fit within the church, we are now in a better position to answer these three basic questions.

The question "Who am I?" is a question of identity. And who are you? You are part of the People of God. Think of it! As a member of

---

[1] Howard A. Snyder, "The Church as God's Agent in Evangelism" in *Let the Earth Hear His Voice*, ed. James Dixon (Minneapolis, World Wide: 1975), 360.

God's people, this means that the biblical story is *your* story. All of it. The Bible is your history, your back story. It is the prologue to your story. And since God's story is the best story ever told, this means that you are part of the best story ever told. Since this is so, how will you live your life? If the Bible and all of human history is just the prologue to your story, the entire universe waits on baited breath for the next chapter. And the question everybody is asking about you is this: "What will you do next?" Since everybody simply cannot wait for the next installment, the next episode, what will you write in the story of your life?

The answer to this question can be found by asking the second question, "Why am I here?" In other words, "What am I supposed to be doing? What is my purpose, role, or function in this life?" The basic definition of church helps answer this question as well. Why are you here? You are here to follow Jesus. Does this sound like a story that will put others to sleep? Have no fear. Following Jesus only sounds boring and dull to those who have not tried it. Again, don't think that you can know where Jesus might lead you by looking at where He has led others. The most shocking and surprising thing about following Jesus is that He leads every single person down a different path. Your path is not my path, nor is my path yours. Every path is completely unique and completely full of surprises around every twist and turn. This is what makes all of our stories so exciting and thrilling. Even the angels long to look into these things. The angels in heaven are binge-watching your life.

This then leads to the third and final question, "Where am I going?" The basic answer to this is that Jesus is leading you into the world. But once again, this is much more exciting than it sounds. Every day with Jesus is sweeter than the day before because every day with Jesus is filled with twists and turns and miraculous events that even the best storytellers cannot imagine or invent. Most Christians, of course, don't experience anything near this level of excitement, but that is because most Christians are barely alive. Most Christians don't experience the life of following Jesus because they wrongly believe they are simply waiting around until they die and go to heaven. Life for them is little more than a waiting game. But Jesus doesn't lead us to a waiting room until our number is up or our name is called. Jesus leads us into the world, to be terrified and thrilled all at the same time. God doesn't want you to die so you can leave earth and go to heaven; He wants you to live so that you can bring heaven down to earth.

So what are you waiting for? You have been raised to new life in Jesus Christ. Your bones have been knit together to do amazing and beautiful and wonderful things! You are part of God's church, God's plan for this world. You have a leading role in the most amazing story ever told. You have been brought back to life so that you can carry forward the story of God. What will you do now? I, and all creation with me, cannot wait to find out.

Rise up, O church of God!
Have done with lesser things;
Give heart and mind and soul and strength
To serve the King of kings.

DISCUSSION GUIDE FOR
CHAPTER 6: "PUTTING FLESH ON THOSE BONES"

Learn more and interact with others who have read this book by accessing the following online lesson:

https://redeeminggod.com/lessons/flesh-on-the-skeleton-church/

Study Questions

1. What church or group of people is your church trying to emulate or duplicate?

2. What are some things your church does that you do not think most of the people enjoy doing? Why is your church still doing these things?

3. Do you feel that your gifts are being used in you church?

4. How do you feel about yourself or your church when you compare yourself to another person or church?

Application: Stop doing Question 4 above. Stop comparing yourself to others. This week, start focusing on those strengths and abilities that make you completely unique. Then focus on enjoying them and putting them into practice. Embrace your unique contribution to the People of God. Be the best *you* that God created you to be, and in so doing, help others find similar freedom as well.

ABOUT JEREMY MYERS

Jeremy Myers is an author, blogger, podcaster, and Bible teacher. Much of his content can be found at RedeemingGod.com, where he seeks to help liberate people from the shackles of religion. He lives in Oregon with his wife and three beautiful daughters.

If you appreciated the content of this book, would you consider recommending it to your friends and leaving a review on Amazon? Thanks!

CONNECT WITH JEREMY MYERS

If you want to read other books by Jeremy Myers or connect with him through Twitter or Facebook, you may do so through any of the following:

RedeemingGod.com
Twitter.com/jeremyers1
Facebook.com/RedeemingGod
Facebook.com/Jeremy.Myers.Author

SKELETON CHURCH: A BARE-BONES DEFINITION OF CHURCH (PREFACE TO THE CLOSE YOUR CHURCH FOR GOOD BOOK SERIES)

The church has a skeleton which is identical in all types of churches. Unity and peace can develop in Christianity if we recognize this skeleton as the simple, bare-bones definition of church. But when we focus on the outer trappings—the skin, hair, and eye color, the clothes, the muscle tone, and other outward appearances—division and strife form within the church.

Let us return to the skeleton church and grow in unity once again.

REVIEWS FROM AMAZON

My church gathering is struggling to break away from traditions which keep us from following Jesus into the world. Jeremy's book lends encouragement and helpful information to groups like us. –Robert A. White

I worried about buying another book that aimed at reducing things to a simple minimum, but the associations of the author along with the price gave me reason to hope and means to see. I really liked this book. First, because it wasn't identical to what other simple church people are saying. He adds unique elements that are worth reading. Second, the size is small enough to read, think, and pray about without getting lost. –Abel Barba

In *Skeleton Church*, Jeremy Myers makes us rethink church. For Myers, the church isn't a style of worship, a row of pews, or even a building. Instead, the church is the people of God, which provides the basic skeletal structure of the church. The muscles, parts, and flesh of the church are how we carry Jesus' mission into our own neighborhoods in our own unique ways. This eBook will make you see the church differently. –Travis Mamone

This book gets back to the basics of the New Testament church— who we are as Christians and what our perspective should be in the world we live in today. Jeremy cuts away all the institutional layers of a church and gets to the heart of our purpose as Christians in the world we live in and how to affect the people around us with God heart and view in mind. Not a physical church in mind. It was a great book and I have read it twice now. –Vaughn Bender

The Skeleton Church ... Oh. My. Word. Why aren't more people reading this!? It was well-written, explained everything beautifully, and it was one of the best explanations of how God intended for church to be. Not to mention an easy read! The author took it all apart, the church, and showed us how it should be. He made it real. If you are searching to find something or someone to show you what God intended for the church, this is the book you need to read. –Ericka

Purchase the Paperback for $5.99
Purchase the eBook for $2.99

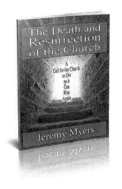

THE DEATH AND RESURRECTION OF THE CHURCH (VOLUME 1 IN THE CLOSE YOUR CHURCH FOR GOOD BOOK SERIES)

In a day when many are looking for ways to revitalize the church, Jeremy Myers argues that the church should die.

This is not only because of the universal principle that death precedes resurrection, but also because the church has adopted certain Satanic values and goals and the only way to break free from our enslavement to these values is to die.

But death will not be the end of the church, just as death was not the end of Jesus. If the church follows Jesus into death, and even to the hellish places on earth, it is only then that the church will rise again to new life and vibrancy in the Kingdom of God.

REVIEWS FROM AMAZON

I have often thought on the church and how its acceptance of corporate methods and assimilation of cultural media mores taints its mission but Jeremy Myers eloquently captures in words the true crux of the matter—that the church is not a social club for do-gooders but to disseminate the good news to all the nooks and crannies in the world and particularly and primarily those bastions in the reign of evil. That the "gates of Hell" Jesus pronounces indicate that the church is in an offensive, not defensive, posture as gates are defensive structures.

I must confess that in reading I was inclined to be in agreement as many of the same thinkers that Myers riffs upon have influenced me also—Walter Wink, Robert Farrar Capon, Greg Boyd, NT Wright, etc. So as I read, I frequently nodded my head in agreement. –GN Trifanaff

The book is well written, easy to understand, organized and consistent thoughts. It rightfully makes the reader at least think about things as … is "the way we have always done it" necessarily the Biblical or Christ-like way, or is it in fact very sinful?! I would recommend the book for pastors and church officers; those who have the most moving-and-shaking clout to implement changes, or keep things the same. –Joel M. Wilson

Absolutely phenomenal. Unless we let go of everything Adamic in our nature, we cannot embrace anything Christlike. For the church to die, we the individual temples must dig our graves. It is a must read for all who take issues about the body of Christ seriously. –Mordecai Petersburg

Purchase the eBook for $6.99
Purchase the Paperback for $8.99

PUT SERVICE BACK INTO THE CHURCH SERVICE (VOLUME 2 IN THE CLOSE YOUR CHURCH FOR GOOD BOOK SERIES)

Churches around the world are trying to revitalize their church services. There is almost nothing they will not try. Some embark on multi-million dollar building campaigns while others sell their buildings to plant home churches. Some hire celebrity pastors to attract crowds of people, while others hire no clergy so that there can be open sharing in the service.

Yet despite everything churches have tried, few focus much time, money, or energy on the one thing that churches are supposed to be doing: loving and serving others like Jesus.

Put Service Back into the Church Service challenges readers to follow a few simple principles and put a few ideas into practice which will help churches of all types and sizes make serving others the primary emphasis of a church service.

REVIEWS FROM AMAZON

Jeremy challenges church addicts, those addicted to an unending parade of church buildings, church services, Bible studies, church programs and more to follow Jesus into our communities, communities filled with lonely, hurting people and BE the church, loving the people in our world with the love of Jesus. Do we need another training program, another seminar, another church building, a re-modeled church building, more staff, updated music, or does our world need us, the followers of Jesus, to BE the church in the world? The book is well-written, challenging and a book that really can make a difference not only in our churches, but also and especially in our neighborhoods and communities. –Charles Epworth

Do you ever have an unexplained frustration with your church, its service or programs? Do you ever feel like you are "spinning your wheels" when it comes to reaching others for Christ? This book helps to explain why this might be happening, and presents a convincing argument for why today's church services are mostly ineffective and inefficient. You will read concepts explained that you've not fully heard before. And you will get hints as to how it could, or should, work. –MikeM

I just finished *Put Service Back Into Church Service* by Jeremy Myers, and as with his others books I have read on the church, it was very challenging. For those who love Jesus, but are questioning the function of the traditional brick and mortar church, and their role in it, this is a must read. It may be a bit unsettling to the reader who is still entrenched in traditional "church," but it will make you think, and possibly re-evaluate your role in the church. Get this book, and all others on the church by Jeremy. –Ward Kelly

Purchase the eBook for $5.99
Purchase the Paperback for $5.99

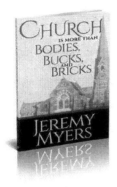

CHURCH IS MORE THAN BODIES, BUCKS, & BRICKS (VOLUME 3 IN THE CLOSE YOUR CHURCH FOR GOOD BOOK SERIES)

Many people define church as a place and time where people gather, a way for ministry money to be given and spent, and a building in which people regularly meet on Sunday mornings.

In this book, author and blogger Jeremy Myers shows that church is more than bodies, bucks, and bricks.

Church is the people of God who follow Jesus into the world, and we can be the church no matter how many people we are with, no matter the size of our church budget, and regardless of whether we have a church building or not.

By abandoning our emphasis on more people, bigger budgets, and newer buildings, we may actually liberate the church to better follow Jesus into the world.

REVIEWS FROM AMAZON

This book does more than just identify issues that have been bothering me about church as we know it, but it goes into history and explains how we got here. In this way it is similar to Viola's *Pagan Christianity*, but I found it a much more enjoyable read. Jeremy goes into more detail on the three issues he covers as well as giving a lot of practical advice on how to remedy these situations. –Portent

This book surprised me. I have never read anything from this author previously. The chapters on the evolution of the tithe were eye openers. This is something that has bothered me for years in the ministry. It may be truth that is too expensive to believe when it comes to feeding the monster. –Karl Ingersoll

Since I returned from Africa 20 years ago I have struggled with going to church back in the States. This book helped me not feel guilty and has helped me process this struggle. It is challenging and overflows with practical suggestions. He loves the church despite its imperfections and suggests ways to break the bondage we find ourselves in. –Truealian

Jeremy Meyers always writes a challenging book ... It seems the American church (as a whole) is very comfortable with the way things are ... The challenge is to get out of the brick and mortar buildings and stagnant programs and minister to the needy in person with funds in hand to meet their needs especially to the widows and orphans as we are directed in the scriptures. –GGTexas

Purchase the eBook for $7.99
Purchase the Paperback for $9.99

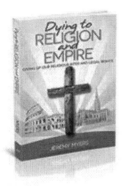

DYING TO RELIGION AND EMPIRE (VOLUME 4 IN THE CLOSE YOUR CHURCH FOR GOOD BOOK SERIES)

Could Christianity exist without religious rites or legal rights? In *Dying to Religion and Empire*, I not only answer this question with an emphatic "Yes!" but argue that if the church is going to thrive in the coming decades, we must give up our religious rites and legal rights.

Regarding religious rites, I call upon the church to abandon the quasi-magical traditions of water baptism and the Lord's Supper and transform or redeem these practices so that they reflect the symbolic meaning and intent which they had in New Testament times.

Furthermore, the church has become far too dependent upon certain legal rights for our continued existence. Ideas such as the right to life, liberty, and the pursuit of happiness are not conducive to living as the people of God who are called to follow Jesus into servanthood and death. Also, reliance upon the freedom of speech, the freedom of assembly, and other such freedoms as established by the Bill of Rights have made the church a servant of the state rather than a servant of God and the gospel. Such freedoms must be forsaken if we are going to live within the rule and reign of God on earth.

This book not only challenges religious and political liberals but conservatives as well. It is a call to leave behind the comfortable religion we know, and follow Jesus into the uncertain and wild ways of radical discipleship. To rise and live in the reality of God's Kingdom, we must first die to religion and empire.

REVIEWS FROM AMAZON

Jeremy is one of the freshest, freest authors out there— and you need to hear what he has to say. This book is startling and new in thought and conclusion. Are the "sacraments" inviolate? Why? Do you worship at a secular altar? Conservative? Liberal? Be prepared to open your eyes. Mr. Myers will not let you keep sleeping!

For all free-thinkers, for all who consider themselves "spiritual," for all who have come out or are on the way out of "Babylon," this is a new book for you! Treat yourself, buy this book and enjoy it! –Shawn P. Smith

Jeremy Myers is one or the most thought provoking authors that I read, this book has really helped me to look outside the box and start thinking how can I make more sense of my relationship with Christ and how can I show others in a way that impacts them the way that Jesus' disciples impacted their world. Great book, great author. –Brett Hotchkiss

Purchase the eBook for $6.99
Purchase the Paperback for $9.99

CRUCIFORM PASTORAL LEADERSHIP (VOLUME 5 IN THE CLOSE YOUR CHURCH FOR GOOD BOOK SERIES)

This book is forthcoming in early 2017.

The final volume in the *Close Your Church for Good* book series look at issues related to pastoral leadership in the church. It discusses topics such as preaching and pastoral pay from the perspective of the cross.

The best way pastors can lead their church is by following Jesus to the cross!

This book will be published in early 2017.

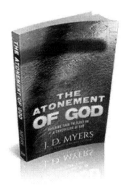

THE ATONEMENT OF GOD: BUILDING YOUR THEOLOGY ON A CRUCIVISION OF GOD

After reading this book, you will never read the Bible the same way again.

By reading this book, you will learn to see God in a whole new light. You will also learn to see yourself in a whole new light, and learn to live life in a whole new way.

The book begins with a short explanation of the various views of the atonement, including an explanation and defense of the "Non-Violent View" of the atonement. This view argues that God did not need or demand the death of Jesus in order to forgive sins. In fact, God has never been angry with us at all, but has always loved and always forgiven.

Following this explanation of the atonement, J. D. Myers takes you on a journey through 10 areas of theology which are radically changed and transformed by the Non-Violent view of the atonement. Read this book, and let your life and theology look more and more like Jesus Christ!

REVIEWS FROM AMAZON

Outstanding book! Thank you for helping me understand "Crucivision" and the "Non-Violent Atonement." Together, they help it all make sense and fit so well into my personal thinking about God. I am encouraged to be truly free to love and forgive, because God has always loved and forgiven without condition, because Christ exemplified this grace on the Cross, and because the Holy Spirit is in the midst of all life, continuing to show the way through people like you. –Samuel R. Mayer

If you have the same resolve as Paul, to know nothing but Jesus and Him crucified (2 Cor 2:2), then this book is for you. I read it the first time from start to finish on Father's Day ... no coincidence. This book revealed Father God's true character; not as an angry wrathful God, but as a kind loving merciful Father to us. Share in Jeremy's revelation concerning Jesus' crucifixion, and how this "vision" of the crucifixion (hence "crucivision") will make you fall in love with Jesus all over again, in a new and deeper way than you could imagine. Buy a copy for a friend—you won't want to give up your copy because you will want to read it again and again until the Holy Spirit makes Jeremy's revelation your revelation. –Amy

This book gives another view of the doctrines we have been taught all of our lives. And this actually makes more sense than what we have heard. I myself have had some of these thoughts but couldn't quite make the sense of it all by myself. J.D. Myers helped me answer some questions and settle some confusion for my doctrinal views. This is truly a refreshing read. Jesus really is the demonstration of who God is and God is much easier to understand than being so mean and vindictive in the Old Testament. The tension between the wrath of God and His justice and the love of God are eased when reading this understanding of the atonement. Read with an open mind and enjoy! –Clare Brownlee

Purchase the eBook for $4.99
Purchase the Paperback for $11.99

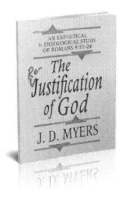

THE RE-JUSTIFICATION OF GOD: A STUDY OF ROMANS 9:10-24

Romans 9 has been a theological battleground for centuries. Scholars from all perspectives have debated whether Paul is teaching corporate or individual election, whether or not God truly hates Esau, and how to understand the hardening of Pharaoh's heart. Both sides have accused the other of misrepresenting God.

In this book, J. D. Myers presents a mediating position. Gleaning from both Calvinistic and Arminian insights into Romans 9, J. D. Myers presents a beautiful portrait of God as described by the pen of the Apostle Paul.

Here is a way to read Romans 9 which allows God to remain sovereign and free, but also allows our theology to avoid the deterministic tendencies which have entrapped certain systems of the past.

Read this book and—maybe for the first time—learn to see God the way Paul saw Him.

REVIEWS FROM AMAZON

Fantastic read! Jeremy Myers has a gift for seeing things from outside of the box and making it easy to understand for the rest of us. The Re-Justification of God provides a fresh and insightful look into Romans 9:10-24 by interpreting it within the context of chapters 9-11 and then fitting it into the framework of Paul's entire epistle as well. Jeremy manages to provide a solid theological exegesis on a widely misunderstood portion of scripture without it sounding to academic. Most importantly, it provides us with a better view and understanding of who God is. If I had a list of ten books that I thought every Christian should read, this one would be on the list. –Wesley Rostoll

I feel the author has spiritual insight to scripture and helps to explain things. I would recommend any of his work! –Uriah Scott

I loved this book! It made me cry and fall in love with God all over again. Romans is one of my favorite books, but now my eyes have been opened to what Paul was really saying. I knew in my heart that God was the good guy, but J. D. Meyers provided the analysis to prove the text. I have been examining all the "proofs" about reformed theology because I was attracted to the message, but couldn't go all the way down the TULIP path, because it did not resonate in my heart that God who is Holy would love imperfectly. I believed Holy trumped Sovereignty, yet, I believe in the sin message, wrath of God, the Gospel and Jesus and decided that I was a "middle of the road" person caught between two big Theologies (the Big C and A). Now, I get it. I can with great confidence read the difficult chapters of Romans, and my furrowed brow is eased. Thank you, J. D. Myers. I love God, even more and am so grateful that his is so longsuffering in his perfect love! Well done. –Treinhart

Purchase the eBook for $2.99

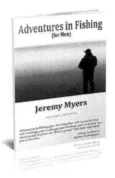

ADVENTURES IN FISHING (FOR MEN)

Adventures in Fishing (for Men) is a satirical look at evangelism and church growth strategies.

Using fictional accounts from his attempts to become a world-famous fisherman, Jeremy Myers shows how many of the evangelism and church growth strategies of today do little to actually reach the world for Jesus Christ.

Adventures in Fishing (for Men) pokes fun at some of the popular evangelistic techniques and strategies endorsed and practiced by many Christians in today's churches. The stories in this book show in humorous detail how little we understand the culture that surrounds us or how to properly reach people with the gospel of Jesus Christ. The story also shows how much time, energy, and money goes into evangelism preparation and training with the end result being that churches rarely accomplish any actual evangelism.

REVIEWS FROM AMAZON

I found *Adventures in Fishing (For Men)* quite funny! Jeremy Myers does a great job shining the light on some of the more common practices in Evangelism today. His allegory gently points to the foolishness that is found within a system that takes the preaching of the gospel and tries to reduce it to a simplified formula. A formula that takes what should be an organic, Spirit led experience and turns it into a gospel that is nutritionally benign.

If you have ever EE'd someone you may find Myers' book offensive, but if you have come to the place where you realize that Evangelism isn't a matter of a script and checklists, then you might benefit from this light-hearted peek at Evangelism today. –Jennifer L. Davis

Adventures in Fishing (for Men) is good book in understanding evangelism to be more than just being a set of methods or to do list to follow. –Ashok Daniel

Purchase the eBook for $0.99

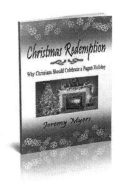

CHRISTMAS REDEMPTION: WHY CHRISTIANS SHOULD CELEBRATE A PAGAN HOLIDAY

Christmas Redemption looks at some of the symbolism and traditions of Christmas, including gifts, the Christmas tree, and even Santa Claus and shows how all of these can be celebrated and enjoyed by Christians as a true and accurate reflection of the gospel.

Though Christmas used to be a pagan holiday, it has been redeemed by Jesus.

If you have been told that Christmas is a pagan holiday and is based on the Roman festival of Saturnalia, or if you have been told that putting up a Christmas tree is idolatrous, or if you have been told that Santa Claus is Satanic and teaches children to be greedy, then you must read this book! In it, you will learn that all of these Christmas traditions have been redeemed by Jesus and are good and healthy ways of celebrating the truth of the gospel and the grace of Jesus Christ.

REVIEWS FROM AMAZON

Too many times we as Christians want to condemn nearly everything around us and in so doing become much like the Pharisees and religious leaders that Jesus encountered. I recommend this book to everyone who has concerns of how and why we celebrate

Christmas. I recommend it to those who do not have any qualms in celebrating but may not know the history of Christmas. I recommend this book to everyone, no matter who or where you are, no matter your background or beliefs, no matter whether you are young or old. –David H.

Very informative book dealing with the roots of our modern Christmas traditions. The Biblical teaching on redemption is excellent! Highly recommended. –Tamara

Finally, an educated writing about Christmas traditions. I have every book Jeremy Myers has written. His writings are fresh and truthful. –Retlaw "Steadfast"

This is a wonderful book full of hope and joy. The book explains where Christmas traditions originated and how they have been changed and been adapted over the years. The hope that the grace that is hidden in the celebrations will turn more hearts to the Lord's call is very evident. Jeremy Myers has given us a lovely gift this Christmas. His insights will lift our hearts and remain with us a long time. –Janet Cardoza

I love how the author uses multiple sources to back up his opinions. He doesn't just use bible verses, he goes back into the history of the topics (pagan rituals, Santa, etc.) as well. Great book! –Jenna G.

Purchase the eBook for $2.99

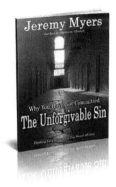

WHY YOU HAVE NOT COMMITTED THE UNFORGIVABLE SIN: FINDING FORGIVENESS FOR THE WORST OF SINS

Are you afraid that you have committed the unforgivable sin?

In this book, you will learn what this sin is and why you have not committed it. After surveying the various views about blasphemy against the Holy Spirit and examining Matthew 12:31-32, you will learn what the sin is and how it is committed.

As a result of reading this book, you will gain freedom from the fear of committing the worst of all sins, and learn how much God loves you!

REVIEWS FROM AMAZON

This book addressed things I have struggled and felt pandered to for years, and helped to bring wholeness to my heart again. –Natalie Fleming

A great read, on a controversial subject; biblical, historical and contextually treated to give the greatest understanding. May be the best on this subject (and there is very few) ever written. – Tony Vance

You must read this book. Forgiveness is necessary to see your blessings. So if you purchase this book, [you will have] no regrets. –Virtuous Woman

Jeremy Myers covers this most difficult topic thoroughly and with great compassion. –J. Holland

Good study. Very helpful. A must read. I like this study because it was an in depth study of the scripture. –Rose Knowles

Excellent read and helpful the reader offers hope for all who may be effected by this subject. He includes e-mails from people, [and] is very thorough. –Richie

Wonderful explication of the unpardonable sin. God loves you more than you know. May Jesus Christ be with you always. –Robert M Sawin III

Excellent book! Highly recommend for anyone who has anxiety and fear about having committed the unforgivable sin. –William Tom

As someone who is constantly worried that they have disappointed or offended God, this book was, quite literally, a "Godsend." I thought I had committed this sin as I swore against the Holy Spirit in my mind. It only started after reading the verse about it in the Bible. The swear words against Him came into my mind over and over and I couldn't seem to stop no matter how much I prayed. I was convinced I was going to hell and cried constantly. I was extremely worried and depressed. This book has allowed me to breathe again, to have hope again. Thank you, Jeremy. I will read and re-read. I believe this book was definitely God inspired. I only wish I had found it sooner. –Sue

Purchase the eBook for $5.99
Purchase the Paperback for $5.99

BOOK PUBLISHING INSTRUCTIONS: A STEP-BY-STEP GUIDE TO PUBLISHING YOUR BOOK AS A PAPERBACK AND EBOOK

The dirty little secret of the publishing industry is that authors don't really need publishing companies any longer. If you want to get published, you can!

This book gives you everything you need to take your unfinished manuscript and get it into print and into the hands of readers. It shows you how to format your manuscript for printing as a paperback and preparing the files for digital eReaders like the Kindle, iPad, and Nook.

This book provides tips and suggestions for editing and typesetting your book, inserting interior images, designing a book cover, and even marketing your book so that people will buy it and read it. Detailed descriptions of what to do are accompanied by screenshots for each step. Additional tools, tips, and websites are also provided which will help get your book published.

If you have a book idea, you need to read this book.

REVIEWS FROM AMAZON

I self-published my first book with the "assistance" of a publishing

company. In the end I was extremely unhappy for various reasons ... Jeremy Myers' book ... does not try to impress with all kinds of "learned quotations" but gets right to the thrust of things, plain and simple. For me this book will be a constant companion as I work on a considerable list of books on Christian doctrines. Whether you are a new aspiring author or one with a book or so behind you, save yourself much effort and frustration by investing in this book.
–Gerrie Malan

This book was incredibly helpful. I am in the process of writing my first book and the info in here has really helped me go into this process with a plan. I now realize how incredibly naive I was about what goes into publishing a book, yet instead of feeling over-whelmed, I now feel prepared for the task. Jeremy has laid out the steps to every aspect of publishing step by step as though they were recipes in a cook book. From writing with Styles and using the Style guide to incorporating images and page layouts, it is all there and will end up saving you hours of time in the editing phase.
–W. Rostoll

Purchase the eBook for $9.99
Purchase the Paperback for $14.99

THE LIE – A SHORT STORY

When one billion people disappear from earth, what explanation does the president provide? Is he telling the truth, or exposing an age-old lie?

This fictional short story contains his televised speech.

Have you ever wondered what the antichrist will say when a billion people disappear from planet earth at the rapture? Here is a fictional account of what he might say.

Purchase the eBook for $0.99

GET UPDATES ABOUT FUTURE BOOKS AND ONLINE THEOLOGY COURSES

Receive updates about future books and online theology courses by joining me at RedeemingGod.com/register/

Made in the USA
San Bernardino, CA
09 January 2019